♪♪Blues For Bill

D1254179

Akron Series in Poetry

AKRON SERIES IN POETRY
Elton Glaser, *Editor*

Barry Seiler, *The Waters of Forgetting*

Raeburn Miller, *The Comma After Love: Selected Poems of Raeburn Miller*

William Greenway, *How the Dead Bury the Dead*

Jon Davis, *Scrimmage of Appetite*

Anita Feng, *Internal Strategies*

Susan Yuzna, *Her Slender Dress*

Raeburn Miller, *The Collected Poems of Raeburn Miller*

Clare Rossini, *Winter Morning with Crow*

Barry Seiler, *Black Leaf*

William Greenway, *Simmer Dim*

Jeanne E. Clark, *Ohio Blue Tips*

Beckian Fritz Goldberg, *Never Be the Horse*

Marlys West, *Notes for a Late-Blooming Martyr*

Dennis Hinrichsen, *Detail from* The Garden of Earthly Delights

Susan Yuzna, *Pale Bird, Spouting Fire*

John Minczeski, *Circle Routes*

Barry Seiler, *Frozen Falls*

Elton Glaser and William Greenway, eds., *I Have My Own Song for It: Modern Poems of Ohio*

Melody Lacina, *Private Hunger*

George Bilgere, *The Good Kiss*

William Greenway, *Ascending Order*

Roger Mitchell, *Delicate Bait*

Lynn Powell, *The Zones of Paradise*

Dennis Hinrichsen, *Cage of Water*

Sharmila Voorakkara, *Fire Wheel*

Kurt Brown, Meg Kearney, Donna Reis, Estha Weiner, eds., *Blues for Bill: A Tribute to William Matthews*

Blues for Bill

A TRIBUTE TO WILLIAM MATTHEWS

EDITED BY KURT BROWN,
MEG KEARNEY, DONNA REIS,
& ESTHA WEINER

FOREWORD BY RUSSELL BANKS

THE UNIVERSITY OF AKRON PRESS
AKRON, OHIO

Copyright © 2005 by Kurt Brown, Meg Kearney, Donna Reis, and Estha Weiner
All rights reserved.

All inquiries and permission requests should be addressed to the Publisher,
The University of Akron Press, 374B Bierce Library, Akron, Ohio 44325—1703.
First edition 2005

08   07   06   05   5   4   3   2   1

LIBRARY OF CONGRESS CATALOGING-IN-PUBLICATION DATA

Blues for Bill : a tribute to William Matthews / foreword by Russell
Banks ; edited by Kurt Brown . . . [et al.].—1st ed.
    p.   cm.—(Akron series in poetry)
Includes index.
    ISBN 1-931968-23-3 (cloth : alk. paper)—ISBN 1-931968-24-1 (pbk. : alk.
paper)
    1. Matthews, William, 1942—Poetry.   2. American poetry—21st
century.   3. Poets—Poetry.   I. Brown, Kurt.   II. Series.
PS3563.A855Z54 2005
811'.54—dc22

                                        2004026941

Manufactured in the United States of America.
The paper used in this publication meets the minimum requirements of American
National Standard for Information Sciences—Permanence of Paper for Printed
Library Materials, ANSI Z39.48—1984. ∞
Cover image: "Waiting," acrylic on pressed tin, 20" x 28",
Scott Kattenbraker, c. 2003
The illustration on pages 1 and 83, "Jazzman," appears courtesy of William
Matthews IV.

Contents

Foreword

Russell Banks

When a beloved friend dies suddenly and unexpectedly ("without warning," as they say, though Bill had given us more than ample warning), one's mind returns almost obsessively to the last time one saw the friend alive. We had met for dinner in New York at San Domenico—Bill's choice, a sleek, dimly lit, *nuevo italiano* restaurant on Central Park South, where the waiters look and dress like gigolos and treat the diners like wealthy, middle-aged, American widows. I hadn't seen him since his life-threatening arterial surgery that summer and expected a much weakened version of the nearly invalid man he'd been the previous spring, but there was, for the first time in a decade, a spring in his step. His cane seemed an elegant affectation, more decorative than orthopedic. His cheeks were pink, and his gray-blue eyes glittered with feisty good health. He'd been off cigarettes for forty days or thereabouts and claimed, typically, that it'd been easy to quit, no problem whatsoever, as if quitting smoking merely hadn't occurred to him before the surgery, or he'd have done it long ago. He wore a new, pale gray, silk jacket and a gorgeous necktie, Italian, no doubt, given the restaurant, and a shirt in a shade of yellow that rhymed with the Bosc pear color of his Bally shoes. His moustache and hair, usually louche and untended, were trim as a suburban hedge, and even his teeth seemed whiter and brighter than I remembered. I think he had new glasses, too.

We drank a harmonic duet of Barolos, ate like minor Florentine aristocrats, and talked that night mostly of the future, because we both believed we still had one. But we talked also, as always, of the past, because we were men in our late fifties and had shared so much of it. Later, we walked up Broadway to Iridium, where we dawdled over a nightcap and took in the last set by Archie Shepp and didn't talk much there, just let our minds and bodies get jostled and groomed by the music and single malt.

We drank our whiskey neat, as I recall, but I would have remembered so much more if I'd known that in two weeks Bill would be dead of "an apparent heart attack." (Bill would have noted that heart attacks are never apparent, except to the heart under attack.) Nonetheless, it was a memorable evening and remains one, and not just because it was our last. We'd had during the previous year a few unacknowledged stress points in our relationship, the type of minor sprains that never cause a break and in lifelong friendships between men are usually fastest healed in silence and in the dark alone. Clearly, on this occasion the healing had been successful, so there was no need to mention the pain, and we were once again closer and more comfortable together than brothers.

We left the club and at the curb on the west side of Broadway grinned and said goodbye. Bill started across the avenue to catch an uptown cab, turned back halfway across, stopped and gave a little wave, then broke into a jog, not to dodge traffic, as there was none just then, but to show me, without having to announce it, that he could jog again, that, for the first time in many years, blood was flowing amply into his legs and lungs, and he could actually run, even when he didn't have to. Watching him, I had that ridiculous, clichéd thought, a fool's thought: Damn! He's gonna make it! And thus when Bill's younger son, Sebastian, telephoned to tell me that his dad, my oldest and most beloved friend, had died, my first reaction was, of course, disbelief. It simply couldn't be true.

I know the biography of the late poet, William Matthews, mainly by memory of how much of it we shared, what he told me of it himself, his sons' and sister's and parents' stories, and the accounts of his ex-wives, all of whom were and still are my friends, which is as much a compliment to Bill as to them. He came from a distinguished, affluent Cincinnati family, its distinction and affluence, by the time he was born in 1942, having been somewhat downsized over the years. He was William Procter Matthews III, but it had been several generations since anyone swimming in his gene pool had been meaningfully associated with Procter & Gamble. He was the elder of two children, went to Berkshire Academy in Massachusetts, did his undergraduate work at Yale in the early 1960s and his graduate work at the University of North Carolina at Chapel Hill in the middle 1960s, leaving in 1967 to teach at Wells College in Aurora, New York, and later at Cornell, University of Colorado, University of Washington, and City College of New York, with brief, sidereal stops along the way at Iowa, Houston, Emerson, and probably a few that I've forgotten. In 1969, while he was still at Wells College, Random House published his first collection of poems, *Ruining the New Road*, poems mostly written while he'd been a student in Chapel Hill. From that point on, there is a public record of his life as a poet, teacher, editor, and as a tiller in the field of literary nurturance with the Associated Writing Programs (president), the National Endowment for the Arts (chair of the Literature Panel), Coordinating Council of Literary Magazines (board member), the Poetry Society of America (president), and a half-dozen other institutions dedicated to the care and feeding of American letters. He became a figure early on, and remained one.

But in this volume of poems and remembrances, he is best remembered as a teacher and friend. He had a gift for both, and he trained, developed, and disciplined those gifts as if they were his precocious children whose talents he could not bear to see wasted. He made teaching and friendship seem easy, as if he'd given them no more thought than he had to quitting smoking. But Bill worked hard at them. Making difficult tasks appear to have been done brilliantly almost by accident was not a point of vanity for him, but a moral principle. Making painful things seem painless, turning evident loss into apparent gain, and converting loneliness into solitude were for Bill ethically necessary. It was *sprezzatura*, a graceful, unspoken way of acknowledging that he was, in effect, one of nature's noblemen, and though he had been born blessed with extraordinary intelligence, talent, good looks, and health and had been given a first-class education and most of the financial and social advantages of a white, middle-class American male of that generation, it was through no fault of his own, and he therefore deserved neither credit nor blame for it. Bill's easy, dismissive grace in the face of difficulty, pain, loss, and loneliness was an ancient and honorable form of modesty.

Bill was the first of my particular generation of poets and writers to die while writing fully mature work, the first to enter the anthologies with two dates after his name and become thereby a part of "literary history." Consequently, long after our personal memories of Bill have gone up the chimney, it's his poetry that will keep him around. Poetry is connective tissue that binds the living to the dead and the dead to the yet unborn. I think of my grandchildren and great-grandchildren reading his poems in a college classroom in some small town (will there be small towns then?) somewhere near Phoenix or outside Lawrence, Kansas, and I wonder, will it matter to them what kind of man wrote those poems? Will they want to have known him personally, to have been one of his students or one of his dear friends or lovers?

Of course, they will, just as I wish I could have known personally all the dead poets whose poems I love and have learned to live by. Perhaps that's the purpose and best possible use for this book of remembrances and elegies, as an intimate portrait of a poet whose poems will outlive all of us who have in these pages remembered his life and mourned his passing. And still remember. And still mourn.

Preface

However else we respond to a person's death—physically, emotionally, ritually—poets also respond to the death of another poet by honoring him or her in words, the very medium in which they excelled and through which they touched and transformed so many lives. Hence, the idea for this book. We had begun to notice the many elegies to Bill Matthews that began to appear during the years following his death, and the many poems dedicated to him, a sure sign of his stature and significance among his peers. The idea occurred to us that such poetic tributes ought to be collected together in one volume that might result in a poetic portrait of Bill, preserving his character, his inimitable spirit and personality as depicted by his fellow workers in the craft.

We began collecting the poems we knew about, the ones we had already read in magazines, and sent out a call for others. Soon, poems began to arrive from every quarter of the country, in envelopes, via e-mail, over the fax. And accompanying them were letters of gratitude and reminiscence. Many felt that a published festschrift like this was in order, that a book of poems about Bill Matthews would make an appropriate shrine to his memory. Others spoke of Bill's gracious spirit, of what a caring teacher and human being he had been, of how much they missed him and loved his work and his excellent company. Phrases of affection abounded with regard to his generosity, his high standards, his warmth and capacity for friendship, his ability to make you feel that he was talking directly to you and you alone. Some expressed their respect for him as a person, and their admiration for his work. All agreed that he had influenced their own work and their lives in various and profound ways.

In his life, Bill Matthews brought many people together. In the same way, after his death we were brought together over a period of many months to discuss the book we had planned, to sift through a large number of poems, to discuss ways in which the book might be structured and designed, to delegate the many and various tasks necessary to compile such a volume and prepare it for publication. We couldn't use *every* poem sent to us, of course, but we wanted to be as inclusive as possible. We are certain that, for one reason or another, there are hundreds of poems about Bill that we never saw, never even heard about, and that many poets whose work deserves to be represented in these pages have been neglected and left out. To these poets we extend our regrets, and hope that they will at least be able to share our joy in this tribute to our mutual teacher and friend.

William Matthews

William Matthews was born in Cincinnati, Ohio, on November 11, 1942. He earned a B.A. from Yale and an M.A. from the University of North Carolina. During his lifetime, he published twelve books of poetry: *Broken Syllables* (Lillabulero, 1969), *Ruining the New Road* (Random House, 1970), *Sticks and Stones* (Pentagram Press, 1970), *An Oar in the Old Water* (The Stone, 1971), *The Cloud* (Barn Dream Press, 1971), *Sleek for the Long Flight* (Random House, 1972), *Rising and Falling* (Atlantic Little Brown, 1973), *Flood* (Little Brown, 1982), *A Happy Childhood* (Little Brown, 1984), *Foreseeable Futures* (Houghton Mifflin, 1987), *Blues If You Want* (Houghton Mifflin, 1989), and *Time & Money* (Houghton Mifflin, 1996), which won the National Book Critics Circle Award and was a finalist for the Lenore Marshall Poetry Prize. A thirteenth collection was published posthumously as *After All: Last Poems* (Houghton Mifflin, 1998). *His Selected Poems and Translations 1969–1991* was published by Houghton Mifflin in 1992. A final volume, *Search Party: Collected Poems*, was published by Houghton Mifflin in 2004.

Matthews is also the author of two books of essays: *Curiosities* (1989) and *The Poetry Blues* (2001), both from University of Michigan Press, the latter edited by Sebastian Matthews and Stanley Plumly.

His translations include *Removed from Time: Poems of Jean Follain*, with Mary Feeney (Tideline Press, 1977), *A World Rich in Anniversaries: Prose Poems of Jean Follain*, with Mary Feeney (Logbridge Rhodes Press, 1979), *The Mortal City: 100 Epigrams from Martial* (Ohio Review Books, 1995), and *The Satires of Horace* (Ausable Press, 2002). He is also the translator of "*Prometheus Bound*," in the volume *Aeschylus, 2: The Persians, Seven Against Thebes, and Prometheus Bound* in the Penn Greek Drama Series (University of Pennsylvania Press, 1998). Many of his translations from the Bulgarian are included in *Selected Poems and Translations 1969–1991*.

Matthews served as president of Associated Writing Programs and of the Poetry Society of America, and was a member and chair of the Literature Panel of the National Endowment for the Arts. He has edited literary magazines (notably *Lillabulero*, which he cofounded with Russell Banks). He received fellowships from the Guggenheim and Ingram Merrill foundations, the National Endowment for the Arts, and the Lila Wallace-Reader's Digest Fund, and in April 1997 he was awarded the Ruth Lilly Prize. He taught at several schools, including Wells College, Cornell University, the University of Colorado, Columbia, New York University, Sarah Lawrence College, and the University of Washington. In addition, he was a visiting poet at Houston, Iowa, and Bucknell. At the time of his death, he was a professor of English and director of the creative writing program at New York's City College.

William Matthews died of a heart attack on November 12, 1997, the day after his fifty-fifth birthday. He is the father of two sons, William Matthews IV and Sebastian Matthews, the latter of whose memoir, *In My Father's Footsteps*, was published by W. W. Norton & Company in 2003.

Sebastian Matthews

Things My Father Passed Down to Me and My Brother

The Marx Brothers
Oscar Robertson
Bob Dylan

The Big Red Machine
       (Perez, Morgan, Concepcion, Rose, Bench,
       Griffey, Geronimo, Foster)

Marley Tosh Stones

Underdog

The ABA David Thompson Dr. J

James Bond Beer Burgers

French Roast Cabernet Sauvignon

Miles
Trane
Monk

Art Pepper Charlie Mingus The Pres and Lady Day

Travis McGhee
Muhammad Ali

Lolita

Ashe vs Connors Borg/McEnroe Jack "the Bear"

Sleeper Love & Death Take the Money and Run

the '79 Sonics   "Hotel California"

Snow Leopards at the Denver Zoo

Rothko Hopper Roethke Hugo Merwin Kinnell

Patrick Ewing   and the Knicks

Easy Rawlins
Tommy Flannagan
Rigoletto

Poems

Cynthia Atkins

Birthday Poem

Lately, every morning I wake
to a death, its length stretched
taut across the hour.
It is a process, pulling
myself out of bed,
if only to find what is loss,
what is gain. Dying
is a private thing.
Bill, did you drop
in the shower fully lathered
and clean for the taking,
one day after your birthday?
I wonder what last line
you were uttering
as steam rose to a contrail
of words. Maybe Coltrane
was hitting a high note
on the stereo, as the cat knocked
a pen off your desk. At that instant,
a ripple skimmed the world.
Someone honked at traffic.
A push broom washed across
a diner floor. The raucous
opera of *grief* and *loss*.
Arbiter, were you the dreamer
the teacher shook the shoulders of?
On a long winter's night
of ink, coffee, snow,
you blew wishes into words
like butterflies lost
in Nabakov's closets.

3

Coleman Barks

Bill Matthews Coming Along

They say the best French wines have *terroir,* meaning the taste of the lay of the land that works through and gets held in the wine, the bouquet of a particular hillside and of the care of those who work there.

When I see Bill Matthews coming along, I see and taste the culture of the world, a lively city, a university campus during Christmas break, a few friendly straggling scholars and artists. I taste the delight of language and desire and music. I see a saint of the great impulse that takes us out at night, to the opera, to the ballgame, to a movie, to poetry, a bar of music, a bar of friends.

When I see Bill Matthews stopped at the end of a long hall, I see my soul waiting for me to catch up, patient, demanding, wanting truth no matter what, the goofiest joke, the work with words we're here to do, saying how it is with emptiness and changing love, and the unchanging. Now I see his two small sons behind him.

Bill would not say it this way; he might even start softly humming "Amazing Grace" if I began my saying, but I go on anyway: god is little g, inside out, a transparency that drenches everything you help us notice: a red blouse, those black kids across Amsterdam, braving the cabs, a nun. You sweet theologian, you grew new names for god: gourmet, cleaning woman, jazz, spring snow.

What fineness and finesse. I love Bill Matthews, and I did not have *near* enough time walking along with him, talking books and ideas, or sitting down to drink the slant and tender face of Provence.

Judith Baumel

Notes for the Elegy

Without   Not yet
But   Still
Because   Unless
Despite   After
However   Within

Your friends—good talker—all
admiration of your talk.

It was the silences I heard, how we
become most ourselves at our boundaries.

In the surrounding silence remain
we who do have rights in this matter

not those late devolving lovers—
tongues cleft to palates.

Body betrays brilliant will
your last quaking quip taught.

A kiss, not yours, at your street corner.
Flesh of lips answered,

muscles of fingers stretched the skin—
that yielding organ—learning.

In all the days of my life since—
in all the nights of my life since—

each *since* a workbook of exercises;
the habit, bad, good, is put on daily.

Jeanne Marie Beaumont

After

All long labors, whether for hunger, for duty, for
Pleasure, or none of the above, one day wrap up.
Put down the itinerant's beaten pouch, pluck no fruit further;
Linger over the melancholy taste of *last* on the tongue.
Even a switchblade wit can't sever another stem.

Plenty is a relative measure—if less than paradise,
It's more than enough. The prolific orchard will, of course,
Continue, other soles trod ladders into the heady
Kingdom of weighted boughs. Insatiable, you might even say
Incorrigible (as though mumbling in winter sleep), the way they can't
Not keep coming back, grasping, tugging, lifting down those
Globes that swell and blush to be handled so.

Marvin Bell

Bill Matthews

The most fluent of poets, Latinate in sneakers—
his third-story study overlooking Puget Sound
was awash in mutual fund reports he never opened.
Bill's nimble, stylish speech defined that household
atop Seattle's Capitol Hill where Sebastian, too,
wrote poetry into the night, the sin and delight in
such avid fluency early demonstrable in the son.

Bill could make a sentence from your best four words,
move you to see the slumminess in it, all while
healing you with wit, affection, and a grace naming
your virtues as he pulled the rug from under
the *poseurs* of the latest poetry fad without spilling
the location of his weaponry or a drop of red wine,
as athletic as Coltrane cornered or Walt Frazier

directing traffic on the court. Bill had a fair jump shot
from the corner, and he boogied with a stamping
as if, and as always, parody were truth itself, a path
apart from the ironists of his generation, for Bill
could chant *It's so easy to fall in love* while hotfooting
to a goofy Bread Loaf Conference lindy,
wildly good-mannered, since, as he explained it,

"If you're invited to dinner, you don't spit on the plate."
The young Bill was quick and willowy, a Dionysian
Donald Sutherland with experienced eyelids,
at times red in the morning after a nighttime of wine,
by which he loosed the savvy, flowing, woven
verse that bore his classic intelligence, brimming
with blood pumped from a politely gasping heart.

7

Earl S. Braggs

Remembering Bill Matthews

When last I saw him, I didn't tell him
I was going to St. Petersburg. I didn't
tell him I'd fallen in love with Akhmatova

and I didn't tell him I needed to see
my reflection in the icy black Baltic.

That evening at his New York City apartment
decorated with classical music, he played
an opera concert, I later learned,
he had planned to attend. At the end,
the night rolled over and I was drunk

on vodka and verse and voice. Yes,
he had a beautiful one. I can hear him now
stumbling through the perfume of visiting ladies.

When last I saw him, I didn't tell him
it was the Stray Dog Cabaret I hoped to find
among the smallest of midnight tables

and light blue circles of cigar smoke. I didn't
tell him about the tragic topcoat Anna
so often wore or the azure shawl she so
carefully placed recklessly over her shoulders,

and I didn't tell him about the fragileness
of her sacred refinement.

That evening in his New York City apartment
decorated with impressions of the Impressionist
movement, we moved out of sync and into
rhythm and blues and magic tragic carefree laughter.

In that city that never sleeps, we slept
wide awake in his voice. Yes,
he had a beautiful one. I can hear him now
ambling from pocket to pocket of his plaid jacket.

When last I saw him, I didn't tell him
I'd fallen in love with Akhmatova. I didn't
tell him I planned to visit the wild and simple country
she refused to leave, and I didn't tell him

I planned to walk the left bank of the Neva,
then through the gates of Great Peter's Summer Garden.

That evening in his New York City apartment
decorated with myth recalling Roman and Greek promise.
The last silver summer before October 1917, I
didn't tell him.

That evening, he cooked Italian pasta poetry.
He recited each boiled spaghetti string line,
each diced perfect onion, each cubed bell, each
sad spin of garlic as if he knew
when I returned from Russia, with or without love,
there would be no leftovers.

Andrea Carter Brown

Blues, for Bill

How fitting that he should come back as blues,
the whole panoply from indigo to ultramarine
on two wings, as cows lumbered up the swale

to a hilltop pasture, the sun sunk behind the now
truly named Blue Ridge, the world in deepening
shadow. How perfect that he should come back

as a butterfly, and yet, given his love of words
and where they come from, how apt it should be
in the blues of a Red-spotted Purple, southerly

conspecific to the White Admiral she might find
in the city where they lived. This is her first summer
in this state; this is the first butterfly she's

ever seen. She is wearing blue jeans. She stands
just beyond the shade of a tall walnut tree,
watching day fade. Except for the cattle, it is

utterly quiet. The butterfly alights on her right hip
and stays, its quivering subsiding slowly to calm.
She could touch it, but doesn't. The Incas believed

warriors fallen in battle visit loved ones left behind
as butterflies, she learns later. She knows very little
of this then. She still doesn't know what happened

to his ashes, his cookbooks and jazz, the last message
she left. She knows where his books went, who took
in Velcro. To satisfy him, she learned the difference

between twilight and dusk. She tries not to budge,
to breathe as lightly as she can. With nightfall, he lifts
off. She knows how lucky she is. How lucky she was.

Harriet Brown

Unfair

All fall I waited for the maple to let go,
and all that fall it stood stubborn,
its crown glowing with green and yellow glory.
You would have said, "Come at the poem
and tree another way." The day I saw
your face leap from the *New York Times*
obituary page, I took my weeping
to the porch and saw the lawn dazzled
with gold at last, as if the maple
had slipped off its gown
after a long, delicious night
and tossed it, crumpled, to the ground.

Years ago I would have written
a lovely sonnet about leaves
transformed to next spring's flowers,
about mulch and its cedary sweetness.
About hope. I would have brought it
to your table, wanting your elegant
benediction, and likely gotten it.
That day I charged into the newly bitter air.
I grabbed the rake and scraped
until the dying leaves were heaped beside the curb.
And when I went inside, red-faced and raw,
I let the front door slam behind me, felt
the rush of blood and rage and doom.
I was alive and you were dead.
I wrote a different poem.

Robert Burr

No Profit

The secretary said, of course, she knew
That it would happen. Hard for her that day,
So many showing up without a clue,
All wanting her perspective. Life's that way.

Reactions, disbelieving, like "Still young,"
"Surprising really," "Too soon, " "So unfair,"
Could not displace the sense of being stung
By her refrain, "Oh, it was in the air."

We'd been up to his house just days before.
He'd conjured Roethke up for us, his class
(Seated, calm-struck, happily on his floor),
While, nimbly, round and through, his cat would pass.

It's hard to think of going, then, as gone,
To mourn the dying limb above the lawn.

Mark Cox

Pissing Off Robert Frost's Porch

Not the side of
a rowboat, granted—
no rising and falling on the wash of tides.
One drink, in honor of you, now dispersed
over day lilies and lupine as the sky Frost knew
resists its darkening, turns slate,
then charcoal grey, an operatic note
held longer than light can hope for.
What we take in, clarify, is temporary;
we pass through each other, heard again
and filtered through the views
to which we're predisposed.
No oceans here, so far from home.
That death's-head moth, I know,
is neither him nor you.
The one candle that draws it forth
belongs, however briefly, to simple me.
And now the dogs express concern,
four or five along the valley's mile.
It will be dark until the earth has turned.
It will be dark now, for awhile.

Stephen Cramer

Before You

How like you, Bill, in the end.
Always the first to explore
whatever hip news chanced
our way—the Sanskrit root
of *chutney*, that backup
bassist with all the right
runs. I bet you were always
quick to stake out
a dive, order a drink.
If you were here,
you'd probably hint
what I'm trying to say
is a bit too much like wine
made from pictures of grapes.
But that last season
I took before you a project
I'd started then stalled on,
& you said this:
take all your doubts,
draw a circle around them,
& give them the finger.
Then you flicked your own finger
from your fist & aimed it
at an imaginary heap
of doubts. So I'm just going
to say it. We miss you.
We miss the sheer velocity
of your presence.
Bill, you beat us out again.
I just thought for once
you'd let someone else
get there before you.

Sascha Feinstein

Matthews in Smoke

All the better that he can walk
from his narrow apartment to the club
now called Smoke, then Augie's,
half the room on barstools beneath
an olive-green mural of alcoholics
so polymorphically depressing
Bill *has* to respond: "Professors Emeritus."
We're in a neighborhood of trouble—
I'm ducking an old girlfriend,
he's ducking a new one—
so when the dour waitress returns
with bad wine and cheap Scotch,
we skip a toast that would translate to
"Good night, night." We're here
mainly out of convenience, so
it's something of a shock when
a chunky tenor player from Chicago—
just twenty-one—saturates the room
with a thick, wet, Dexter Gordon tone.
In two years, he'll be known
(second place in the Monk contest,
the best near-win in jazz history),
but now he's swinging "Bewitched"
as a *waltz,* the lyrics—"I'm wild
again, beguiled again"—spun in thirds
across the high hat's steady shimmer.
The kid's making notice, and Bill forsakes

witty references, unveiled allusions,
triumphant alliterative punch lines—
he leaves them all in the bar's tip gutter.
Tonight, it's the real thing, music
putting language not to shame, exactly,
nor in its place. Tonight, language
burns faster than Bill's cigarettes.
Tonight it's all "Holy shit" and "Oh yeah."

Allen C. Fischer

Inspiration

When they took your body to be cremated,
I thought of history's renegade clans
burning books, cleansing minds,
creating a zealot's tabula rasa.
But as I imagined your dreams
disintegrating, their lines going up
into the invisible literature of space,
I sensed that all might not be gone.

For if landscape is light taking shape,
then your unwritten poetry may be wind
caught listening, looking for substance:
the cursive that swallows dart,
the map outlined on a maple leaf,
how waves wrap their quests,
or the calming mantra of distant
mountains after a long day.

In the streets and out in the fields is
a poem emptied of its material.
I think I heard you this morning
high in a hemlock, found
your humor in the pond's ripple.
As you put it one evening
during a meal heavy with metaphor,
"This potato is full of itself."

Debra Fried

Untitled: For Bill Matthews

The street stirs, yawning, awake
and out of the morning's emptiness.
Already a small crowd is hurrying,
fruit is set out on the stands, and the edge
of a paper flutters upward, weighed down
by a sole, veined stone.
How relentless life seems in its eagerness
with the sting of your death present.
The poems I sent stand on my shelf,
flaps torn where I opened letters
or once even a scrap of paper
as you spoke them back to me,
your practiced hand black in the margins.
For a time, time was suspended
in that decayed cathedral,
the glove someone chalked on the pavement
where worlds crossed and Sterno fires burned,
the familiar steep walk uphill
past the stoops of tired apartments
cavernous even in daylight,
and the ball field—huge, deserted—
its fence ripped open
as if by a fist.
In that embattled place,
you taught what you knew best:
that the poem is its own reward
for loss, for imperfect life,
a truce with what possesses us,

with what we can't control, as the massive
force of flood
leaves evidence of its being, tokens
by which it is known
long after its departure.
What you might say—that grief
is tempered by a music
true to all the strangeness of self,
its form as real as body?
My letter bears no stamp,
the streets no sign of you
this cruelest month. *Neither
father nor lover,* but guide
to lead us gently out
of hell, if hell were silence.

Rachel Hadas

The Last Time

Some people ambush you
and stop you in your tracks while at their pleasure
they tell you their endless story.
Others stamp right past you and ignore
your presence inches from their frozen face.
And others glide, they slope
around a corner, wry, amused, alert.

When I was last in Bill's vicinity,
we happened to be standing side by side
studying complex little mechanisms
(apple corer; tea ball; garlic press)
at Lechter's Housewares, where, for me, the old
Moon Palace's scar had yet to heal.
Still, there we were, intent in the same aisle,
absorbed as museum goers
halted before a single masterpiece.
We talked, predictably,
of flavors, kitchens, stores, the neighborhood,
and parted with a pair
of casual waves, vague but reciprocal.

And that was the last time.
But in what sense the last?
Not the last time the worn
Confederate soldier face,
the drooping mustache and distinctive limp
rose in my mind's eye. On the contrary.
So in what sense the last?
His passage left a ripple in the light.

Daniel Halpern

The Eternal Light of Talk

That's one way to look at it, I thought,
without naming it, leaving the thing
unnamed, without definition—still,
just beyond, breathing but silently.

Well, he would have thought of it that way,
too. A passing on of language, like the gift
of one of his beloved oxymorons, like
famous poet or *living will* or *sure thing,*

or a bottle of his favorite bargain Bordeaux
to accompany one of his famously elaborate meals
compiled of unlikely ingredients—
like his palette of language.

Or late into the evening, to himself,
it might have been a passing *through*
language to the other side, a landscape
no longer requiring hip and knee for transport.

And over there, if there's foie gras, he's found it,
and when he found it, he found a way
to import the right Chardonnay to keep it company.
I never met a sweetbread I didn't love, he would say,

sipping slyly on a rare, woody white isolated
on a sudden mission to the West Coast.
He had a life he kept even from himself.
I never heard him utter an interrogative.

22

Why be surprised by the unknown?
We made it a point to toast the life
we seemed to be leading
wherever we found ourselves.

Who else would so intuitively name a cat Velcro?
Or love Mingus and Donizetti with equal vigor?
The vocabulary for solace is impoverished.
To be sure, his was a living will.

James Harms

Sleek for the Long Flight

Rain in quick eighth notes
made Broadway a brief
song, the shower passing
east into Queens
like a curtain drawn back.
The taxi was humid
with breath and
the heat from our hair:
Paige and Noelle
on either side of me,
David by the driver,
you giving directions
as you leaked
cigarette smoke out
the inch of open window.
You'd only heard
about the restaurant,
a silly hybrid of Tex-Mex
and Italian, ethnic dining
run amok on the Upper
West Side. And you couldn't
promise anything, though later,
not even the strange
confusion of food
could sap your love of what
was hidden there,
the three or four stray
herbs in the salad,
something wrong
with the sauce that made it
different, you said,
and almost good.

Pamela Harrison

Magic Lantern

The chairs were hard.
The room was hot.
A poet of his stature
might have been forgiven
for being brief.

Our motley band
of hopeless and ambitious
lovers of his craft
crowded in a crescent
toward the brilliant, unscripted
speech that fell with such aplomb
from his mustachioed mouth.

With a comedian's flawless timing,
he focused the magic lantern of his mind
on mastering foul shots and jazz riffs,
his reflection so gently trained
on all our failures it seemed
we merely overheard a genius
musing to himself.

Wasn't that the magic of the man—
candor joined with kindness
for everyone but himself?
His shirt, when he was done,
was soaked—the only sign
of what those words had cost.

Walter R. Holland

The Poet Speaks of Italy

Your book of Sicily with dog-eared edges
Like a Baedecker on its last legs, plied through the rains

Of Rome in November. So you catalogued a dinner's delights—
Satyricon of the senses, in an alcove near the Piazza

Navonna. The untraveled in me wanted your poet's
Phrasebook of words, your rich voice saying *"Dove? Dove?"*

Salted cheeses and oil on tomatoes, the simmering broth
Of crusted shrimps and the harbor's calamari, inky black,

Pounded on rocks until the softened tentacles were dropped
In vats of boiling oil, battered flour turned brown.

Of course, sea salt was tossed from the cook's dark hands—
"I wonder where he'd put them during the day—the wife always smiling."

Describing the Fiat's shaky ride, the broken cliffs, the autumn light.
You talked of food, *scioperi,* wines, the reds served dark

And ribboned. Like Dante seeking Virgil, I sought your
True advice on the dominions of the earthly and the pure.

The way you led us all with your lantern—irony—shining at the edges
Of self-disclosure—the *colto, divertente* American.

"But drink the grappa! No cheaper ticket to oblivion—it will make even you
a counter-tenor! Paradise comes soon enough, after all, with check and cappuccino."

Dove? Dove?: "Where? Where?"
scioperi: "strikes," as in transit strike
ribboned: wine forms a film on the sides of a glass, called "ribbons," which reflect sugar content
colto, divetente: "cultivated, amusing"

Ann Hurwitz

Bill at Bellagio: A Rockefeller Grant

Whoever trims the topiary,
kneads the dough, brings round the mail
creates a frame to hold a life
of ease. When Ella Walker walked
the garden paths at Villa Serballoni,
servants hid behind the cypress trees
so she might think the garden's beauty
hers alone and happenstance. Here's
something to consider—the economic
structure and where the poet fits.

"I'd won a month's work," the essay begins
("essay" which means to test or weigh
and from its derivation, a weighing,
hence a balance). The work
he planned to do was write,
repair a broken heart, and fight
despair at incapacity
to get the heart work right.

The labor here is meant to be
unnoticed. And so *"The stimuli
just don't come in."* He's fleetingly
awake to lizards, imagines an opera's
drama in his head, stuffed and drunk
with wine from Serballoni's grapes,
but not without a qualm. In fact
his lungs are full of qualm's black smoke.

The dinner talk of these, mostly
unmoneyed, men and women, tentative
at first, takes off and turns around
the cost of each one's visit and recent

renovations made to make their stay
still more exquisite and thus, the theory
seems, more artfully productive.

Bill lights up and takes a drag.
Behind his half-closed eyes, he thinks,
"Suppose . . . the object
of work, in addition to whatever
specific need it addresses,
is to be done with it, to reach
what we . . . call leisure. And suppose further
that leisure is not a commodity, ... , an end
in itself, but the oxygen of art."

Ah! Here's the trick, the one he's mastered
so completely it's hard to see the skill,
the work behind the work,
the thing he says makes art of value, that is,
the way he pulls the ropes, keeps sorrow
wafted off the ground surrounded
all around by air.

Envoi

In a dream of Bill last night he names me Writer
although I rarely write and hands me a gift,
three ashtrays, like shallow votive basins,
which he instructs me to nail against the wall
and fill with ashes. "Burn paper," he says, "and end
procrastination," something grief
is a species of, according to the words
of Samuel Johnson whom he quotes.

Richard Jackson

Reincarnation of a Lovebird

*What's wrong with money is what's wrong with love;
it spurns those who need it most for someone already rolling in it.*
—William Matthews

Already it is snowing, the branches spattering out of darkness
the way I imagine the nerve endings of that grasshopper
did on my sill last summer while the nightingale finished it.
Already old fears condense on the panes with you
a thousand miles or words away, my friend
recently buried, the light in my room blaring all night
the way it's done in prisons, trying to keep too much emotion
from scurrying out of the corners. There's a blind spot in
the middle of your eye, the guilt you feel for loving so fully
in the face of death, or dying in spite of love's power.
These verbs are searchlights for memories gone over the wall.
It's all we can do to embrace the distance between us
while night limps across the rooftops, while we preside
over the heart's fire sale. Outside the streetlights hook
a reluctant sky. Memory won't save everything.
The nightingale disappeared into the piracantha bush
to flute a melody we call imitation but may only be
another lie. Charlie Mingus's bass would die
into an arrangement, then reincarnate itself as a form of
love. It's time to decide if this is an elegy or a love
poem lurking behind one of the smoked glass windshields
that go up or down the street every few minutes. What we
should have said to each other waits like an insect
all winter for a false spring. The language of stars
no longer brings consolation or love. The Egyptians
invented the phrase "eat, drink, and be merry,"
you know the rest, but kept a skeleton
hung at dinner parties in case you tried to forget.
My love, the heart taps its way along sidewalks
like a blind man, and muggers are gleeful on the corners.

What we need are more emergency vehicles for the soul.
We need to knock at the door of the heart's timekeeper.
The tracks I'll leave later when I go out into the purity
of snow will destroy it. The scientist's light
on the atom alters what should be there.
Every glass we raise we eventually have to lower.

Jacqueline Johnson

Last Class

On this particular Sunday,
your cat Velcro jumps
on my shoulder. You look at me,
surprised: "She never does that
to strangers. She must like you."

Your apartment is filled
with normal addictions: books,
bread, wine, women, and jazz.
In the background, soft drone
of voices giving critique.

How you manage to tell us
the poem is both terrible
and possible in the same breath
is a marvel. Your level gaze challenges.
We are gallows poets sure to hang

without a glimpse of perfection.
A few fleeting hours later,
we walk out of your apartment
single file. In a faded black
and white marble hallway,

I look back to see a man
dressed in a blue shirt
under a striped sleeveless sweater.
You are fragile, thin,
your gray eyes strangely fixed.

For a moment, I glimpse terror
on that weary, reddened face.
You have chosen to show me
how much you hate loneliness,
you, who have left no joy unspent.

Rodney Jones

The Secret of William Matthews

Once he wryly admitted, "I write for friends"—
He was one, but distant—a card from New York
When he bested two dead poets to win a prize,
Shrugging off his laurels, "Stiff competition!"
Though he set those words in a lover's mouth.

Just think of what fun he'd have with these—
"For friends," he said, as though interlopers
Didn't crouch at the margins of those odes
He liked to make to jazz, sex, wine, and food,
Parodying the lucky roll of a shooter's touch.

More like he was lifting the roof of a house
To expose not just pleasure but pleasure's
Underside: his natural double-take—one hand
Warning fellow revelers, "Don't wake daddy,"
While the other cranked up the volume.

Now the body in the work is his, as promised:
There's irony as proof of mythic embarrassment—
And slippery craft and cold technique,
For his music had evolved from the scalier
Anatomies of friendliness and married love.

I see him dapper in a sportscoat, wreathed in smoke:
One of a generation that refused to grow up,
Or the master addressing his too-short remarks
(Confidentially and to whom it may concern)
With that blues grace, that singing that talks.

Meg Kearney

Nature Poetry

Bill hated the separation implied by the term.
"What's *this*?" he'd ask, gesturing toward what lay
beyond our classroom window. From "NAC" 6—303
in Harlem, Manhattan blinked and glowed like
a floor of stalagmite, lit by its own desire
to exist. What was it? Concrete, glass, steel—
meaning limestone silica, gypsum, sand,
manganese, sodium sulfur, ore—
anything unnatural here? Here in the city, we
steel ourselves against the elements—steel,
from the Old High German *stak*, "to resist"—
and we fight like the animals we are for our
own little plot of privacy amidst all this
concrete (from the Latin, *concrete-us*, past-
participle of *con-crescere*, "to grow together").
We're too much together, and all the while we
go around like Adam and put a name to things,
just to say *this is real, I exist in this world.*
So we say "boulevard," "taxi," "skyscraper," "villain"—
which used to mean you worked on a farm, but now
means you better have eyes in the back of your
head walking down the boulevard. "Be careful going
home," Bill would say at the end of the class. "It's
a jungle out there." Yes, we'd agree. Naturally.

David Keller

My Blue Heaven

"Ah, all the elves are at the toyshop," he said,
looking up as he approached the porch,
meaning, I thought then, to refer to the others
as mischief-makers, revelers, fellow weirdos,
which, of course, they were, and he was, too,
and flashed us a look of expensive laughter
so eloquent only a clown or child could've done it.

Like money, he kept us in circulation.
His lines dazzled and we clapped our hands
with delight, full of envy and joy
at what he could do. So much we didn't know
how to say, or to avoid saying,
he put into words for us like an amused parent
helping the kids with an assignment.

Each poem seemed both new and familiar
as the girl of our dreams, who is, he remarked
once, the worst possible woman to marry,
and we did anyway, and didn't he
know it, didn't he ramble, didn't he?
What could you expect from someone who dealt in
"stand-up tragedy," as he thought of the art?

With him seemed to go whole jazz recordings.
Nights of music he liked to think of
himself as part of, playing chorus
after chorus on one number or another,
suddenly ceased to exist, vanished, gone,
as if he'd only conjured them up, while we
thumb through his books, hoping to find traces of them.

36

Now we patrons at the bar of the Flattened
Heart, each left fumbling over old songs,
turning over memories like small change,
we will have to learn how to get on without him.
And why not? We have each other, of course,
and our own self or two, that constant
companion to be true to, if we cared
or could remember how. Why not? All the elves
are at the toyshop. All but one.

Gerry LaFemina

Elegy for William Matthews

On television one of those shows with angels who have nothing
better to do than help us humans out, and in the store
angel figurines—some plucking harp strings and some blowing

celestial trumpets. I can't help but think of Gillespie then.
Can't help but think of Miles. Really, though, I think of Matthews
in his Upper West Side apartment with a record spinning,

followed by another. The whole time he was discussing one
poem or poet, but occasionally he'd stop and point something
out: a particular riff, maybe, or the vibraphone

player, the rhythm section. If I could, right now, I'd apologize
for the hokey angels that began this poem,
but he'd probably forgive me for that. I hadn't realized

the last time we talked—a phone call about meeting for drinks
in late November when I'd be in New York next—
would be the last time we talked. That's the funny thing

about death, for those of us left here with our horns
still wailing. The first time we met, he drew a wine glass
above his signature in *Foreseeable Futures*, and when I mourned

for him that long December, I read his books as if for the first time,
delighting in their sounds and caesuras. Now, years later,
I've been celebrating his kindnesses with an editor, glasses of wine

raised, deep red in the light. I'd like to think the slight beat of glass
against glass is the sound he loved, or at least enjoyed. Back at home,
I spin a record in his honor: Gillespie blows "Swing Low Sweet Cadillac."

Peter Makuck

Last Call

He answered the phone uncertainly,
long distance dark between us,

and the sound of caught breath,
wheezing, then a drawn-out silence.

I asked if anything was wrong.
He coughed and said he'd been alone

in his apartment all day, watching
the snow fly, listening to jazz,

feeling something slowly grow inside.
"Your phone call did it," he said.

"When I opened my mouth just now,
a huge hawkmoth fluttered out."

I knew better than to ask further.
I see it still beating at the overhead light.

Gary Margolis

Writers' Conference

Although you were the master
    teacher, you invited us, your fellow
and scholar—poets-in-training—
    to be part of conferences with your

conferees. *More is likely to arise in
    threes,* you said, and, sitting in the Barn,
Bread Loaf's living room, it's true,
    we could keep six eyes on who

walked in with whom, in between
    comments about a line's slack
or where an image like gossip
    lacked surprise. We couldn't

remember who said two heads
    are better than one, but somehow
you knew it took three of pharaoh's
    architects to plan the granary at

Thebes, even though it didn't rain
    enough for the grain to be roofed.
But it did rain frogs. And from that
    thought, at the end of one of those steamy

hours, it began to rain on the slate barn
    roof, on August's slightly turning leaves.
Not rain yet, you said, but something else
    that is and isn't. Not mist and almost drizzle.

You translated the dots and dashes etched by
    our poet-scribe-to-be, and said
we shouldn't be afraid to read those smudges
    or walk out into the rainy mizzle.

Cleopatra Mathis

Over a Long Distance

The Port from which I set out was the port of my loneliness.
—Henry James

Before I found the sea,
you waved at me from the little bridge
over that little river, the Gale, all the chattering
eddying water, the backdrop that claimed my voice
up the mountain road's show—torn butterfly,
blackberry and lily, while you

changed the light with a word.
Ocean water hides its turmoil, opposing
currents meet and part, too fast
along the uneven bottom.
But your charmed calm, your gaze
crossing mine—

easy to wade out over those stones, to accept
my reflection in the brilliant surface of your elegance.

Sebastian Matthews

Buying Wine

When we were boys, we had a choice: stay in the car or else
follow him into Wine Mart, that cavernous retail barn,

down aisle after aisle—California reds to Australian blends
to French dessert wines—past bins loaded like bat racks

with bottles, each with its own heraldic tag, its licked coat
of arms, trailing after our father as he pushed the ever-filling cart,

bent forward in concentration, one hand stroking
his unkempt mustache, the other lofting up bottles like fruit

then setting them down, weighing the store of data in his brain
against the cost, the year, the cut of meat he'd select at the butcher's:

a lamb chop, say, if this Umbrian red had enough body to marry,
to dance on its legs in the bell of the night; or some scallops maybe,

those languid hearts of the sea, a poet's dozen in a baggy,
and a Pinot Grigio light enough not to disturb their salty murmur.

Often, we'd stay in the car until we'd used up the radio
and our dwindling capacity to believe our father

might actually "Just be back," then break free, releasing
our seatbelts, drifting to the edges of the parking lot like horses

loosed in a field following the sun's endgame of shade; sometimes
I'd peer into the front window, breath fogging the sale's signs,

catching snippets of my father's profile appearing and disappearing
behind the tall cardboard stacks. Once I slipped back into the store,

wandering the aisles, master of my own cart, loading it to bursting
for the dream party I was going to throw. But mostly, like now,

as I search for the perfect twelve-dollar bottle, I'd shuffle along, dancing bear
behind circus master, and wait for my father to pronounce, tall

in his basketball body, wine bottles like babies in his hands, "Aha!"

Karen McCosker

Request

At the other end, a door opens:
disembodied pleasantries, delight
in his most recent success.

Apology . . . *a few friends here* . . .

I am a stranger requesting
something for nothing:
a poem for an anthology.

Long-distance gate-crasher,
I await the gracious
brush-off, a more convenient
time to call . . .

Instead, a poem is sent,
of *hayricks* and *cuckoos*,
and the cage we make of ourselves
when we close our door
on the uninvited guest,
when we have nothing good left to say.

Christopher Merrill

Bill

As in a statement of particulars—
A drooping mustache and an aching hip;
A penchant for bons mots and rumpled shirts;
A *stand-up tragic,* as he liked to say.
Dead at the age . . . The author of . . . Survived by . . .

As in to issue or announce, to touch
And rub, to caress—women, words (*Good, Bad,
Right, Wrong*), a glass of wine. Another glass?
Don't mind if I do. And then the lights
Went out, and so we never saw the end

Of the empire, a novel might begin,
In which the solos of his stand-in, a blind
Jazz drummer hopelessly in love with smoky
Bars and the rhythms of America,
Separate light from dark, the wheat from the chaff.

As in a formal petition (*obsolete*):
To language, say, or to the gods of misrule,
Time, and desire, which coaxed from him a blues,
A body of work to replace his own
Stiff joints and remorse, revising, then revised.

As in the jaws of the peregrine falcon,
The "cosmopolitan" perched on the skyscraper;
The point of an anchor digging into sand;
The visor of a baseball cap. As in
The check. Check, please. The tip's included. Thank you.

Judson Mitcham

Some Words for Bill Matthews

Those cold eyes aimed our way made it clear
we had laughed too hard. You proposed
words for the look that she had given us:
mirth control, you called it.
                              And today,
when I thought of that quip once again,
remembering how *silly,* in an early sense, meant
blessed in the spirit, I had gone out
shopping for a used car.
                              Everywhere I went,
they were calling old heaps *pre-owned,*
as though a service had been done:
they had pre-worn the brake pads down, pre-bent
the fender, pre-replaced the alternator;
they'd pre-built the clutch.
                              So each of us
is used; we're all vehicular: the word
takes us for a spin.
It honks the horn, violates the laws, gets us lost,
and trades us in.
                              The motor of the old new car
gave a low smoker's laugh
as I drove it off the lot this afternoon.
The jazzy bad news buzzed the radio. The road
moaned its only tune.

47

Robert Morgan

In Memory of William Matthews

A veteran insomniac,
if you had ever slept, you could not
have read so much and thought so much
and written so many pages.
Even awake, the rest of us
were never as awake as you.
I was in awe of your alertness
and your articulateness. I've
never met another who talked
so long and well. Tradition meant
a lot to you. You were a connoisseur
of wines, of things Italian, of
custom shoes, who would forget
to match or even to wear socks.
Of our generation you were the most
generous behind the mask of irony.
What's there to say now you are dead?
You were both old before your time
and younger than the rest of us.
That meant a lot to me, that
and your enthusiasm for words
and your quick snarls about the nature
of nature poetry. Bill,
wherever you are now, I'm sure
you're laughing at the way we poets
take ourselves so seriously.
And I concede the fault, except
I want to say I took you seriously
and was not wrong. Your death keeps on
astounding me with jolts of sadness,
as I think I'll never hear your voice

again or get a letter filled
with needled gossip. The book is now
both closed and open, the last
dinner and last jazz savored
in the fine hours over brandy
and smoke that hung like incense in
a Hindu temple everywhere
you lived. I want to note that you
were loved and that your work is loved
and will be. That's the final flower
I bring to lay at the place of
memory, even as I hear you snicker
beyond the veil of silence: send
no flowers, bub, but maybe some
good claret might not be unwelcome.

Sharon Olds

Matthews Ah Um

Dear Bill, on the pavement to your service, in the gingko
oak muddle of the night's storm,
a tiny tulip shone, one piece
of metal confetti, as if coming up
in November through cement. And in a gutter, wound
with dark leaves like hair, a pink
toothbrush. Are you packed? Do you have your hanky,
have you got your keys? A trio of people came toward me,
laughing, taking up the whole sidewalk,
I wanted for them to be removed rapidly
so I could walk without swerving, but then
I thought, as if you broke out in me in a
riff, *Joy takes precedence*
over sorrow, Kiddo, so I veered around them, in
close to the Orthodox Church, her porch
mossed with tiny, pink, paper
hearts. Any of us who has failed in love
might feel ashamed to be alive and well
when Bright Star and you are parted,
not that I'm offering to take your place,
Not this pig—life line we would toss
between us, who were raised as if intended
to give up to others, and did not want to
and didn't. But then you learned the bright-star
language, the earliest human tongue,
pure love's licks like and unlike
a mother's cleaning of her own inner
foods and debris from the newborn's mouth
and eyes. By the curb, shards of gold
reflector, standing in its craquelure
two old couples and two young cops,
and near the funeral home, a tall

handsome man, making music with coins
in a cup. From my pocket, a dollar of our sorry
republic, his eyes a lot like yours
and mine, Bill, afraid and proud
and humorous. I think you would have
liked the service, your gifts and virtues
praised, your flaws praised as virtues,
as if we have all drunk bright star
and can sing for an hour. At the end, when the horn
went up and cried out, we couldn't tell
his wails from ours, in those phrases the brilliant
brass, massed tears, fresh flowers, swam
and murled. Until that moment, I had thought
a person *was* his flesh—when Galway had
said, They took the body to Bellevue,
I had thought, No, they took Bill
to Bellevue. But now I saw I had been wrong,
the skin of your coffin silken, the grain
musical, the hidden burl,
structural power. Dear Bill, up
above the bole, as if from the tree
you sing, now, in perpetuity.
You came naked from your mother's womb
shrieking and wincing, you leave the earth
rich with song, gleaming with new love's knowing.

Rick Pernod

Fixity

Tobacco-cured wool and scuffed Italian shoes,
that (make sure you get the exact word, Rick) *premonitory*
smile, the pause, then launch through the crystal palace
of eloquence, six feet of language so quick,
dazzling, in the flow of our consideration.
You rode your brilliance like a rodeo star,
unselfconscious, a bit reckless, always able
to hold on to the reins a few seconds longer:
the sheer exhilaration of insight.

The other graduate students called you Bill,
but I called you Professor Matthews, even though I was forty
and by far the closest to you in age.
I was from the Bronx, a degree from the University
of Minnesota, in sociology of all things—former busboy, caddy,
kiln operator, Yellow Pages salesman, bartender,
and now, budding poet on the cusp of middle age.

The first time I shakily read
a poem in class, one of your obviously more
seasoned students said how many "rules
of thumb" I had violated, and you said you would never
let thumbs get in the way of vitality.

Professor Matthews, I promised myself I would not hit
the false notes of sentiment. Let me instead state what
I have learned: to stonewall the phonies, to applaud
the finely rendered, that fear and sloth are the
enemies of excellence, and to look
in the mirror when the lights are on.

52

I never got to show you my final thesis.
The last time I saw you I said I was
worried if it was going to be good enough.
You said I should worry if it was *just* good enough.
A few days later you were dead.

Thank you for never asking me to call you Bill.
You knew *professor* was the exact word I needed there.
These days, I've been listening to Wagner's *Tristan and Isolde*.
The fat lady is singing, Professor;
she knows Tristan's not coming back anymore;
she knows it won't be long before
the curtain drops.

Oh sing, sing your sweet ass off, good mother:
it's never any good
unless we know
it's going to break our hearts
after all.

Stanley Plumly

When He Fell Backwards Into His Coffin

The rumor, because we all want to die happy,
is that he was in the bath listening to Verdi.
Probably singing, too, or mouthing with the masters.
So it must have hit him hard, the surprise faster
than a fall on ice or the missed step off a sidewalk,
his mouth opened wide in order to talk
himself out of it. The truth is he was resting
on the edge of an empty tub, fully dressed,
every cell, body and soul, beginning to annul
every future cell. And whatever he was thinking, solo,
a capella, he must have had a moment,
as memory voided him, that he remembered, as he'd told it,
how his mother held his head down in the bath
to tease him or test him, or both.

Donna Reis

Following William Matthews' Recipe
for Scallion Risotto

Who else but you
would state what kind of white wine
to add to the Arborio. . . .

I sauté the scallions in olive oil,
and keep them from browning
with a dash of dry Pinot Grigio.
Attentiveness to detail
was your secret ingredient.

Well, not so secret,
it was always there for the tasting
like the stock of poetry you boiled down
to a thick paste and spooned
into our gluttonous mouths.
Stick with it, you said.

The first time I met you,
I imagined your long, aristocratic body
leaning against a wall at a cocktail party
swirling a glass of wine
as a student soaked up your words
so she could savor them again and again.
I stir the rice
till it becomes creamy with wine.
You nudge my elbow,
Come on now,
add another half cup of broth,
as you pushed us
to simmer language until each line fattened.

We remove the pan from the heat,
stir in the remaining two tablespoons of butter,
the green scallion tops, cheese, and white pepper.
You feign a swoon as you relish the first taste.
How like you to write
the servings as: six as a first course;
four, if the guests are polite, for an entrée.
How this dish warms me
like the poetic endings you described
that jump up and give you a big wet kiss,
then slip you a ten dollar bill.
How much you are missed.

Kenneth Rosen

Matthews in Maine, 1980

Portland, Maine's great conversion of harborside warehouses
        And dying storefronts into law offices
And enlightened speakeasies—hippy entrepreneurship, America
        Giving birth to itself, once again, as . . . *A*M*E*R*I*C*A!*—
Was in full convulsive bloom, and in a tavern on Congress Street,
        In bright blue-gray daylight, the color of Matthews'
Irises, I was swilling wine with famous poets and publishers,
        Trying to find by brave sycophancy

Pieces of the puzzle I believed I was missing. A *doppelgänger*
        From the bar, hair flopped over his brow
And a movie-star moustache, asked us for a cigarette, then
        A match, and wandered back to annoy two girls
With behinds as firm as their bar stools and pretending
        They were cleverly preoccupied. My gang
Wondered who he was? A novelist? An actor? A famous rival
        From a distant sphere? "Nice suit," observed

Matthews, sipping his martini, nudging with the cavalier's
        Fringe on his lip the yellow frill on his olive's
Toothpick. "Rumpled shirt," I interposed sourly. Matthews
        Lit his own cigarette, gazed across his shoulder,
Exhaled a reflective plume, and looked at me trying to figure
        Something out. "Good eye," he said at last,
"Good eye." And that was the man's genius: he was urbane,
        And knew that everyone was good for something.

Vern Rutsala

We Never Shot Baskets Together

Back in the days of *Lillabulero*, we
sent letters back and forth,
and I remember saying that a poet
he mentioned was a second-string

Simic. In his answer I could almost
hear him chuckle—that laugh
I came to know those few times we met—
as he nudged me towards his view.

I now think he was right—maybe—
but that talent to sew a chuckle
into a sentence—that was something!
Somehow feeding it into the pace

of his words and showing a tough
fairness as well: As if saying, I know,
I know, but we're in this shit together,
and we need each other, a little.

Later he suggested my name
for a panel somewhere, and I
thanked him, and he said—that
chuckle again—you may not thank

me when the time comes.
But he was there in the audience,
smiling, sad eyes carrying their
own news, echoed somehow

in the droop of his mustache.
We never got to shoot baskets
together—a quick twinge
that surfaced just now. I wonder

how good he was. Probably
solid, a good passer, ready to
set you up for an easy two,
but expecting you to be ready

with your head in the game.

John Schenck

Open to Everything

"To the second-best writer I know,"
he scribbled on the title page of my copy of
Blues If You Want.
Try to imagine something more flattering.

"What it sets out to accomplish,
it does very well," he said
of an especially unambitious poem
I had just read in his workshop.

At Yale, he tooled around
in a sporty Datsun Fairlady.
Bill doted on the car, although
its name taxed his urbanity.

Despite an ostensible lankiness,
Bill was paunchy, not a graceful athlete,
but he'd play the occasional pickup game.
He moved well, for a poet.

He loved the subversive.

In his workshop the week after he died,
we tried to decide if Bill made us feel
inadequate or brilliant.
Some were awed by his intellect;
others empowered by his equable openness
to even the most awkward stanza.

In fact, he was open to everything,
and shared what he found.
Trockenbeerenauslese, for example.
Not so much the wine
as its Teutonic tumble of syllables.
His recipe for pepper shrimp
is on the menu tonight,
and though I've never quite penetrated
the mystery of Mingus,
I'm open to it.

Dave Smith

Coming Down in Ohio

My uniform hung Air Force blue, way uncool,
when we first met, but Italian silks fit you
sleek as a summer shower. Tall and thin,
Gauloises, Yale swagger, you were the rule
exceptions were made to break. Years unkind,

to say the least, wiped out that grin I still see
when you lounged like Rimbaud, poet maudit.
Blonde coeds drooled and took notes.
You quoted Horace, charmed us, sipped chablis
like gospel, cooed over Monk, bloomed in smoke

killing Hugo and Wright, lungs flagged black.
Thirty-something, you sagged by noon, the slack
red set eyes, stride gimpy, stiff—
that was exactly what you lived to enact,
a boy-poet, rich as Dickens, keelhauled by life.

The more you aged, the more booze, pills, crunch
of poets got you. No jazz played too much
or kept the night-fears off. You loved one
woman for looks, one art, one touch
as cool as grace you envied and easily took on,

praising fingers of NBA centers or of pianists.
You ranked these only lower than trumpets.
You played some yourself, slow forward
I recall, and argued game as well as any theorist.
Watch his elbows, Plumly groaned. I'd been warned,

and still you swiped my ball and nicked my face

enough to let me know the penalty of place
applied anywhere we played with lines
exactly. The last time I saw you, you laced
up shoes, chair-bound, breathless, sweating in sun.

Then you died. I took it hard, as if you were youth
my friends and I expected to keep, half-tune
half-heard, like being sealed in a heartbeat
that dribbles, surges, leaves you stooped.
Memory plays hard when we turn rank as meat.

Maybe that's why I can't read unguarded elegies
where, almost, you walk on water. Silly.
I'm in a photo with you gone in for a lay-up.
Your hand's near the rim; beneath your feet,
there's only air, asphalt, and nothing to disrupt

what looks, given this angle, perfect and casual.
Just the way you liked things. Dusk, marginal
as a zone, holds the rest of us stunned.
See, our mouths are open as if we sing choral
tributes as you rise, sexy star, razor-quick, alone.

Understanding how hurt scores, you always clowned.
Here you grin, float, beating our shouts
"you're out of time!" The photo's pale,
but your look's locked on the ball as down
your body comes among us, who cry foul, most foul.

Henry Taylor

For William Matthews

If nothing ever happens more than once,
we still think we know enough to entitle us
to a few expectations, and to love

those moments when anticipated pleasures
strike us sweetly numb. How many times
you felt and spoke the exact way it was

to be in a room where musicians worked
toward those rare and swiftly fleeting
convergences of everything there is,

the world honed down to what vibrated
between your glass and the cone of light
in smoky air where sorcery kicked in

often enough to keep you coming back.
One time in Washington, it was you
the light picked out at an elevated podium,

your head tilted a little to one side
as if you were listening and speaking at once,
eyes sometimes closed, the soft voice

grazing carefully over lines and sentences,
and it came to me that if I had the power
to keep you around and turn you off and on

at will, as if you were a radio,
I would have all I need of what I get
from writing poems, and could quit.

It might be so. Slavery's illegal,
and now you are gone. I still like telling it,
bringing back the realization of that moment

to meet the disbelief or faith it might arouse.
I believe it. Like the tunes you wrote about,
your poems do not so much bring back a time

as lift us out of this one toward another
that has never been, not yet, no matter
how hard we might wish it had been, however
much about it comes just close enough.

Melinda Thomsen

Ode to Bill's Vocabulary, 1997

Now the whole earth had one language and few words
—Genesis 11:1

Hubris, laconic, indolence, shriven,
bathetic, pelagic, impervious, feral,
primeval, unctuous, and quixotic,

which I noted, he mentioned on two
occasions, dropped from his mouth
like the pages of a dictionary his own

teacher had breezed past his head
before hitting the wall and collapsing
into a mop of wings. Bill had smiled,

at the taste of his "perfect metaphor."
Later, opening the *Scarlet Pimpernel*
that cost me ten cents at a church fair,

the edges of its dry text dissolved
into an orange powder at my fingers'
touch. I read fearing it would vanish

before I knew what a pimpernel was
and started my love of collecting, too.
My previous attempts, first with shells

then insects, failed. I was quickly bored
with the Connecticut mollusks or moths,
an offering of extremely pale versions

unlike anything in *National Geographic*.
Now, I display an array of vocabulary
like cabriolet, phaeton, barouch, cutter,

brougham, and hansom with no need
to dust them off or mount with a pin
through the thorax before placing them

next to their meanings. Bill's words
were an endless runnel of edifying
gifts, even on November eleventh

when he used "interiorities" twice.
Would he shake his head that sad
way today at my ignorance while

I look up "liberty" and "freedom"
like I did when he said "epithalamium?"
At a writers' conference, I remarked

that the definition of "duende" was
"the power to attract through personal
magnetism and charm," but was told

that "that was the Webster's watered-
down, sugar-coated version of duende."
Just the same, when my Random House

binding split, I couldn't just discard it.
The three parts I've saved as guards,
stationed at the ready.

Richard Tillinghast

Glimpse of a Traveller

A stranger with a Sunday to kill
Before flying out of Shannon,
He stands at the bar in the Old Ground Hotel
In jeans and a Savile Row jacket,
Drinking a black-and-tan,
Writing in a notebook he takes from his pocket.

He looks well against the background
Of dark walnut and stained glass.
Above bricky pouches, his eyes comprehend
The life that circulates just beneath the surface
Around him. Foam from his pint clings
To one of his moustache's lopsided wings,
But he takes no notice.

Surely there was a boy here once
With parents, schools, summer camps, and crushes,
And his own ways of destroying his innocence.
It's hard to tell what flinches
His handsome deadpan features mask.
Is he a ladies man or a family man
Adrift? You'd have to ask—
If you ever lay eyes on him again.

Sidney Wade

Bill Matthews, 1983

*"You must release as much of this hoard as you can,
little by little, in perfect time, as the work of the body
become a body of work."*
—from "Mingus in Diaspora"

Drink, the great modifier,
grips the tall lanky frame
in its joyous fist
and places it gently
in the midst
of a student party
where it bobs and grins,
not a lampshade,
but a lengthy light pull cord
encircling the head,
like a skimpy
Indian headdress,
or the cotton string
of wisdom's seeker.
There is a radiant,
confused heart pumping
inside the beanpole body,
rising and falling
to a perishable beat
in the dark middle
of a stranger's living room.
Its rhythms will carry
the body forward,
this delicate instrument
we all use
to play our poems.
He knows so well
the Latin music,

and all that jazz
composed by other vivid
parties before him,
and bit by bit
adds his wonderful own
to the great body
of the world's poem
till many years later
the fine heart will fail
this smartest
and most charming
of finite forms.

Bruce Weigl

Elegy for Matthews

The best long flight
I saw you sleek through,
late summer,
late evening in Penn Station,
the white
Casablanca suit
I'd seen you wear
that same morning,
splattered now with your blood.
I watched you too long
for the sake of goodness,
or for the sake of
even the most simple
kind of grace
we may manage.
I watched you
across the station
move your hips
to the funky music
from a box
some kid rested
on his shoulder,
your formerly
impeccable suit
covered with your dried
and your drying blood.
What hasn't been lost to me,
even now,
is the way that you
walked through that hubbub
after our eyes had met
across the distance between us,

stride of the fox, or maybe
stride of the clever dog,
until you were right there,
before me,
where I felt the generous
light of you again.

I asked your bloody suit
what had happened
with my eyes,
and without a moment's
hesitation
you said you'd just auditioned
for a part
in a Brian DePalma movie,
and then you
smiled that way you did
inside the place that exists
between the kiss
and the last breath
where you had loved
to dwell.
When you told me
the story of your bleeding,
I did not want to take you
up in my arms
and make it stop.
I wanted to run away.

Estha Weiner

On the "Island of the Old Women,"
in the middle of Loch Lomond,
I wander
Inchailloch Burial Ground,
on vacation
from the year of the dead.

Whoever cared
has placed a wooden bench
for the visitor
to sit amongst the gravestones,
one from Clan McGregor,
"family" of Rob Roy, "Celebrated
Highland Rogue," another
educated pirate.

Some gravestones offer
symbols which do honor
to the crafts
of the people buried here:
sheep, scythe, and sword,
but no symbol for a poet,
called in Scots, "makar,"
"a skilled and versatile worker
in the craft of writing."

I wish you were buried
on the "Island of the Old Women."

I wish you were buried
anywhere with a place
for words. Instead,
your incomparable talent
to disappear
at will . . .

Bill, tell me
if this poem's finished.

David Wojahn

Scrabble With Matthews

Jerboa on a triple: I was in for it,
my *zither* on a double looking feeble

as a "promising" first book. Oedipal & reckless,
my scheme would fail: keep him a couple drinks

ahead, & perhaps the muse would smile
upon me with some *s*es or some blanks.

January, Vermont: snowflakes teased the windows
of the Burlington airport bar. The waitress

tallied tips & channel-surfed above the amber
stutter of the snowplow's light: it couldn't

keep up, either. Visibility to zero, nothing taking off
& his *dulcimer* before me (fifty bonus points

for "bingos") like a cautionary tale. The night
before I'd been his warm-up act,

the audience of expensive preppies
doubling to twenty when he shambled

to the podium and gave them Martial
& his then-new poems. "Why do you write

something nobody reads anymore?" queried one
little trust fund in a blazer. "Because

I'm willing to be honestly confused
& honestly fearful." *Il miglior fabbro,*

a.k.a. *Prez*: sweet and fitting honorifics he has left
upon the living's lips. Sweet & fitting, too,

that I could know the poems much better than
the man, flawed as I am told he was. Connoisseur

of word-root & amphibrach, of Coltrane
solo & of California reds, of box scores & Horatian loss,

his garrulousness formidable and masking
a shyness I could never penetrate, meeting him

would always find me tongue-tied,
minding my *p*'s & *q*'s, the latter of which

I could not play, failing three times to draw a *u*.
The dead care nothing for our eulogies:

he wrote this many times & well.
& yet I pray his rumpled *daimon*

shall guide our letters forward
as they wend the snow-white notebook leaves,

the stanzas scrolling down the laptop screens.
Game after game & the snow labored on.

Phalanx bourboned whiteout & the board aglow
as he'd best me again & again. *Qintar*

& *prosody*, the runway lights enshrouded
& the wind, *endquote*, shook the panes.

Susan Wood

In Cortona, Thinking of Bill

No wonder you loved this country, place
of civility and pleasure—you were a connoisseur
of both, those stays against the poet's sickness:
a strain of terminal sadness. It could kill us all
in the end, I guess, though you wanted to deny it
in the worst way. And how bad was that?
Let me count the ways you dressed up
your grief: music, especially jazz, and basketball
—all sports, in fact—and poems, of course, and food
and wine, and travel anywhere. Don't forget marriage,
that most confusing stay against confusion yet—
you tried three times, officially, and more. And always,
always wit—too glib sometimes, I thought,
and you agreed—but a mind sharpening
and sharpening its knives. It was your heart,

though, that brought you down in a cloud
of smoke, like Auden's making "a last fist"
and fighting back, punching your lights out,
while water meant to revive you after a long day
swirled over bathroom tiles, sluiced down the drain.
Your coat lying on the bed and opera tickets in your pocket
—I don't know, but I like to imagine it was *Turandot*,
the opera Puccini left behind unfinished at his death,
though there was no *diminuendo* of his powers.
Or maybe *Tosca*: the tenor—he's an artist—
about to die, singing *"E lucevan le stelle,"* and then
reprieve, and oh, the joy, the reunion with his love!
But no, it's all a cruel trick—the guns
have bullets in them. These are ironies

you'd have appreciated, I think, taking the long view,
like this one, for instance, from the terrace at Tonino's,
the whole Valdichiana coming to light. Lake Trasimeno,
far off, a silver cup on a silver plate, and on the blue hills,
sunflowers winking on like millions of lamps. And the light
itself, liquid, gold, oil poured from an olive grove.
This morning I've been reading your book,
the posthumous one—how hard it is to say that.
You didn't believe that "Auden died
because his face invaded his body," as someone said,
that the best suffer most and it shows, but here you are
looking out from your book, your face in its gravity
longer than shadows on the wall behind you,
bags under your eyes deep enough to hold a world
of tears. I can hear you giggle at that—
you had a nose for self-pity, especially your own—
it stank to high heaven. It's not suffering
that eats us, you said, but our own bad habits.

Later I'll walk home slowly up the steep hill
by the peach-colored hospital, the day already gone
slack with heat, home to the lax hours of books and naps.
Then evening, with its *passeggiata*, the already familiar
faces filling the piazza, while in front of Bar Signorelli
the town's rich widows gossip at their favorite table,
nursing Campari and sodas and comparing their lovers—
young men from the country said to visit late at night
when all the town's asleep. Such civility and pleasure!
And then, the swallows diving and swooping
over the piazza at dusk, or hovering over
the tall houses, the ones with the small, second doors
only the dead can pass through. Those birds remind me
of angels in Luca Signorelli's *Nativity*—Luca,

local boy made good—angels hovering over the body
of a tiny, oddly ancient Christ Child. At night
they gather on the roof of the hospital—
Santa Maria della Misericordia, Saint Mary of Mercy.
How much you loved what words do, and defy,
and how close they are, our suffering
and what saves us.

Baron Wormser

Melancholy Baby

You sit at the end of the bar
Beneath the basketball game
On the TV. The people look at you
Partially, which suits your permanent mood.
Though it's a different bar tonight,
You order the usual. Contemplating too long tends to
Bring on a triple shot of trouble.
Something exciting has happened in the game;
There's a briefly fervent look in people's eyes.
You peer into your drink. It's no Sargasso Sea,
And you're no diver. There's something akin to joy
In being so world-weary.

You walk into the funeral home
And announce yourself as a business
Associate because we are all business
Associates in America even if
We high-mindedly try to ignore it or join
A transcendent cult or just blisslessly screw up
On what seems like our own.
The fact is for so punctilious a presence
Time has some pretty irregular habits
Like someone who has a lot of old
Dry cleaning slips in the bottom of her purse.
Where is that beige wool coat?
Time doesn't return any calls, then pulls
The phone from the wall jack, hurls it through
A closed window, and stomps out of the apartment
Muttering, "It's forever, you flesh-and-blood fucker, it's forever."
Grief wants some air freshener.
The coffin glows like an old-moneyed smile.

80

You sit down on a folding chair in the last row
At the poetry reading. A man is decanting
His ironic ambitions. A woman is throwing exquisite
Knives at her hapless childhood. It's not so much
Enlightening as recklessly appalling.
You can respect that.
The art of diceyness lays some rigorous odds.
Afterwards the patter starts up again
Like an election campaign or machine,
But how else could it be?

You lie awake and polish some words.
You never know when you might want one of them.
In your blue eyes, there are no reprobates.
All moments are pickled in this
Ingenuous, articulate brine.
It's neither reassuring nor unkind.
Everything will be open again in the morning.
You might sleep sometime.

Interview

An Interview with William Matthews

David Wojahn and James Harms interviewed William Matthews in the living room of his apartment on West 121st in New York in October of 1995. The interview took several hours.

Wojahn: *Although you grew up in the Midwest and had a childhood there that seems a bit akin to those of Stanley Plumly and to some extent Philip Levine, you don't go back to your Ohio and your upbringing with the same sort of mythic urgency which they insist upon. Myth for you seems to reside more in the imaginative life, in literature and jazz especially. Home for you seems to exist most crucially in art, in the delights of being an impassioned reader, listener, and fan. Do you remember the first time you were moved by something you read, or by a piece of music you heard?*

Matthews: I don't know if I remember the first time. It is certainly the case that for me home is an invented place and not a given. And to a certain degree is, therefore, without geography. It is true, though, that often when I dream, if the dream is set out in a landscape, it resembles southwestern Ohio. I'm not sure you can reprogram dreams to do anything but that. Home is a place that has to be constantly imagined and peopled, a place where you are not bored, one might say. What I have in common with Phil Levine's Midwestern childhood is not, I think, particularly Midwestern. It has to do with downward mobility . . . or sideways mobility. Maybe Phil's is more downward. What feels similar to me is a refusal to accept the comforts of the situation we were brought up in. Something that may contribute to this is the fact that I was born in '42; my father was in the Navy. I was a war baby and lived part of my childhood with my grandparents, and then part of my childhood in a succession of places with my parents. My sister came along three-and-a-half years after I did. So there isn't one prevailing physical place that I could regard as home, and that may make it easier or more urgent to invent a sense of home. I don't know what is Midwestern in all of that, but Phil and Stan both have, and I probably do, too (but I can see it less well in me than in them, just because we don't see ourselves very easily), a certain desperate Midwestern friendliness. There may be a link here.

Harms: *How did your childhood contribute to your being a poet, or didn't it?*

Matthews: Well, it had to. And, of course, the unfindable needle in the haystack has something to do with the notion that what everyone agrees to be the most formative years are the years upon which an obligatory amnesia falls. The first two years of your life are the crucial molding period, says everyone. And nobody can remember almost anything about this period, which actually makes it very easy to make big assertions because no evidence to contradict them is available. This seems to me the strangest thing, in some ways, about being human. This period about which we all have a strong intuitive sense, which is so incredibly important, is absolutely unavailable.

But anyway, in my earlier years, I lived in somebody else's house, and though my grandparents were very affectionate and treated me like a little prince in some ways, it still wasn't my own house. They were older than my parents and were very fond of children, rather sentimental about them, even. But they'd had children around for a lot of years, and I was near the very tail of the kite. I had a lot of time on my hands there, too, so entertaining myself became a survival skill. And later, when I was living with my parents in the early years, we lived in the country. My father was a county agent for the Soil Conservation service, a Department of Agriculture employee. He did that for the first twelve or thirteen years of my life. We always lived at the edge of town or outside it. You would go out to play and there were corn fields and a dog and the weather. And you had to invent something to make that landscape interesting, less stark. And, of course, later on, this inventiveness became the very kind of thing for which you were punished: promiscuous curiosity, daydreaming, staring rudely out the window. These were the skills we discovered to our great pleasure but which our teachers told us could never be useful at all. But our teachers, of course, were wrong.

The other thing to be said about childhood is the way in which it encourages you to think of the imaginative life as being in some important way a real life, and not an opposition to or an escape from anything.

86

If you sat in a corner and sucked your thumb, people started wondering if the school psychologist should be consulted. If you sat in a corner reading a book and pointedly ignoring everybody, that was the sign that you were a good child. There were a lot of rewards from reading. You could go on long excursions away from the house and the family by just sticking your nose in a book.

Harms: *Did the interest in music start just as early?*

Matthews: It came a little later. I grew up in a house with records but not in a house where people just sat and listened to music. I am perfectly capable of sitting for three or four hours at a time and listening to music and not uttering a word during that time and not doing anything else (not reading or doing some other thing). And nobody in the house listened to music like that. But soon I discovered that it was like reading. It had great private rewards, and it meant that I was being a good child. When I got into my early teens, I was interested already in classical music, and what I liked most was baroque, Bach in particular. Bach through Hayden was my golden age. And there were a couple of radio stations that you could get late at night that played what was still called race music, where you could listen to Black rock and roll and its forerunners. Then life began to get interesting. It also meant you could occasionally hear a little jazz on the radio.

Harms: *When did the transition into wanting to make your own art happen?*

Matthews: Well, I took piano lessons when I was young. I was never sent away to camp in the summer, and I wasn't trucked out for a series of lessons (like soccer), not like a certain kind of suburban kid who takes every lesson and participates in every sport. I did play little league baseball because I liked baseball a lot. My father was a fan and played amateur ball into his late thirties. He was a catcher and managed a local team. There were some evenings, when I was kid, when we sat in the bleachers in some ball field and watched these aging ball players scuffle. So, it made sense that I was going to do that. I think I probably asked for piano lessons. And that drizzled off. Later I took clarinet lessons, and I stayed with that a little longer, but I wasn't good enough. You figure that out fairly early on, it turns out. Your fantasies of what it will lead to are corrected by the fact that it doesn't lead that way: there is that one little Mozart sonata that everybody can play, and then comes the time when you have to do the second one. And then you realize that you are going to have to display technical things that you don't possess yet. If you're really good, what it leads to is the pleasure of learning that, and that leads to the pleasure of learning the third thing, which is even more difficult. You're not sitting there picturing yourself on the cover of *Time* magazine. You're thinking, "You know, in another couple of months, I could really do one of the late sonatas." When you're not good, it doesn't lead anywhere except to the next lesson. It's pedestrian and purgatorial. Probably the highest thing a musical career would have led me to was the chance to teach students as indifferently skilled as myself.

Wojahn: *How was the pattern of discovery different when you started writing poems?*

Matthews: I wrote a few poems in high school and a few in college. And for the usual reasons: I was either incredibly sad or wanted to impress a girl. I really didn't start writing poems until I was out of college, and then as a kind of prophylactic against graduate school. I was a graduate student in English lit., and I came to dislike it—not English lit., but graduate school per se. It was a dreadful choice. I had no idea why I could have done something so foolish to myself, that displayed so little self-knowledge. Better to start writing poems than trying to solve insoluble problems like that.

So I started teaching myself to write poems—I never had a creative writing class. Yale, like most of the Ivy League schools, disdained teaching creative writing. When I started to teach myself poetry writing, I found that the process I couldn't make happen in music was somehow available to me through writing. I could write a poem, which made it possible for me to write another poem, and then another poem. When I started, I wasn't thinking of putting a book together. I started writing poems and loved the quality of attention it drew from me, and I loved the activity. I just kept writing poems and, at a certain point, I thought,

88

"Maybe I'll do something with these." But what I was really interested in at first was simply the way curiosity rolled out in front of you like a rug before the beginning of a cartoon. And it just kept working.

Wojahn: *Why don't we talk about your first book and your early work? Those poems seem very rooted in some of the period styles of the '60s and '70s, the short imagistic poems of Merwin and Wright, Bly, whom you've written about in your essays. How did you get attracted to that sort of writing, to the Deep Image writing that was in fashion then?*

Matthews: It happened to me in the way it did for a lot of poets. Yale also didn't administer courses in very recent poetry; courses didn't go much past 1945 or so. I didn't really have much idea about what was out there, but I started buying books and reading stuff that other people around me were reading. I had never read Roethke's essay, "How to Write like Somebody Else."

It took me about two years to begin reading Roethke in any form. If I had, I might have figured out that it could be interesting to systematically imitate somebody. What I did instead was to imitate the zeitgeist. I wrote in the period style. It had one advantage for me—the prevailing poem was short and heavily metaphorical. The short part was the biggest advantage. When you're trying to teach yourself how to write, one of the things you invariably want to do is go on and on. But my poems were short because it was what I could manage. It takes a while to teach yourself to keep on going. I wrote poems so very short that they seemed to begin and to end almost simultaneously. I thought I could make something in which structural integrity was possible, as long as the scale was comparatively small. And that if I did enough of that, I could learn to go on longer. I also have a metaphorical imagination or bent and had one even as a child. The idea that the making of metaphors is a kind of thought process had occurred to me in some natural and untheoretical way at a fairly early age. I thought, "This doesn't feel dauntingly difficult." It was more difficult than I first thought, but it was something I was able to do.

Harms: *Starting with those early models, did you feel fairly quickly that you were part of something, of a school or a movement?*

Matthews: Well, yes and no. I liked James Wright's poems a lot, for reasons I didn't understand at the time. I liked Merwin's poems a great deal. It took me a while to realize that one of the things that interested me about their work is that it is always composed by someone learned and well-educated who has figured out a way to write without wearing that. Two of the poets of my own generation [whom] I ran into back then were Robert Morgan and Charles Simic. Robert was living in Raleigh in those years and used to come over to visit me in Chapel Hill. And I was sent Simic's first book and then reviewed it for an early issue of *Lillabulero*. I was attracted to a lot of things in their work, but I didn't feel a part of a movement in any important sense, and I didn't have the same enemies. I was too naive literarily to have any enemies, though I may have been reacting unconsciously to my rather Augustan graduate experience in the Yale English department.

Wojahn: *I'm just thinking, when you bring up Merwin and Wright, of how the interest in those short, subjective, surrealist poems also starts to manifest itself in your work in the interest in the epigram. Horace was Wright's favorite poet, and I know he is one of yours.*

Matthews: Always. And I can think of a couple of similar poets, not contemporaries, who interested me a great deal as a reader when I was young but [whom] I didn't know how to make any use of in writing my own poems. I'm thinking especially of Auden and Byron. I came to feel some temperamental rhyme with them as a reader very early, but I didn't know enough literature then, nor how to write well enough to make any particular use of them as models. I was also reading Stevens at that age. I thought, "I know this guy is terrific, but I don't understand these poems yet, so I am going to turn my back on his work for a while and come back to it when I have a better chance of figuring out what I can do with it." I set a number of writers aside on a to-do-later, when-you're-grown-up shelf.

Harms: *The method of Deep Imagism that you employed in your first two books seemed to have run its course by the time of your third book,* Rising and Falling, *in which you seem to find a different voice. The poems change considerably.*

Matthews: I don't know how much of that change was conscious, but a lot of what seem to be aesthetic decisions, particularly if you take a narrative interest in your own life or career, are really made on a much more inarticulate level than that. For me, a major thing that happens is that I get bored. You write a number of poems that have certain things in common, and, after a while, you have begun to solve whatever problems have been presented to you by a style, a form, or a subject. You get to the point where you pretty well know what you are doing. As I near that point, I get bored, and I get eager to get stupid again and to take on something that I don't know how to do yet.

In the case of *Rising and Falling*, I think the change was dictated by a subliminal sense of that. Also, there was a new set of subjects I was interested in writing about. A lot of Deep Image poems were about the assumption that subject matter is a stand-in for something else. In that sense, they are Freudian and see themselves as having a latent and a manifest content, though I think Jung may be the presiding theoretician for those poems rather than Freud. But there is still a sense that the poem is the vehicle to get at something which is unspoken or unspeakable, something beyond its surface content. But that view is not one I share. I think of poems as engaging subject matter in order to produce something which isn't subject matter and that really is *poetry*. For me, at least, I need subject matter in order to write. Andy Warhol once invited Mingus to come out to East Hampton to discuss making a film. Mingus had written the score for Cassavetes' film, *Shadows*, and it was a big hit among the hip. So, he went out to East Hampton, and he kept saying, "So, what are we going to do?" And Warhol said, "Well, we're going to improvise." After about a day of this, Mingus went off in a huff. And he could go off in quite a huff, given his size and authority. He said to Warhol, "You can't improvise on nothing, man." For me, subject matters are like chord changes; they are not what poems are about, but there is something about subject matter—as there is about memorizing the chord changes to a really beautiful song—that allows you to get to the thing which isn't subject matter in the poetry as much as it is a kind of *transmutation*. But it's not about something which is not said. Art is the thing that you make *out* of the chord changes or the subject matter.

In that sense, engagements with subject matter were very important to me. But Deep Imagist poems seem to me, on some level, queasy about having subject matter and treat their subjects as a kind of distraction—the way Language Poets think of certain kinds of plot as the opiate of the masses, which you have to get rid of in order to find out what is really going on in a poem. For me, the subject has never been the point, but it has always been the vehicle.

Another cause of the change in style is that the first two books came out in 1970 and 1972, and then there was a pause while I retooled. During the period, I got divorced and contrived to bring my children to live with me, not during the summers but during their school years. I had to deal with the consequences of and responsibilities for a divorce. And I had to deal with my own children, which drove me into a more urgent, considerable curiosity about childhood than I would have had on my own. It meant moving a couple of times. The things that mattered to me a lot in my life, that I wanted to be able to write about so that I could be as smart about them as I could be and possibly even smart enough to stop trying to be smart about them, were about wanting very much to do a good job raising the kids, and figuring out how it was that I found myself in that situation, which in some ways had the same kind of awful rhyme for me as the decision to go to graduate school—which seemed like such a wise decision and then suddenly was insupportable. I had a marriage which I had entered with every optimism and affection, and it went sour within a short period of time. And I thought, "I have done this again; what is going on here? You can't be this ignorant. You need to know something you don't know."

I was beginning to figure out that poems were a way of thinking. It seemed natural to want to write different kinds of poems under a different set of urgencies, poems that had people in them and social consequences and that were about different experiences with time and that were about loyalty and betrayal. I needed to be able to address all those things—not by a series of explicitly autobiographical poems. There is not much of a paper trail, though anybody reading those books would know that there are two male children very much at the heart of the author's life. Questions of what home is and isn't are very important, but other than that, there aren't autobiographical poems about divorce fights. The facts are not there. They are the dull part anyway.

Wojahn: *What often happens in* Rising and Falling, *and also in later poems like "Whiplash" and "Bystanders," is an engagement with narrative. They are poems that start with a lengthy anecdotal piece, but they seem very much a variety of cautionary tale. It is as if you tell the stories to warn us or remind us about human folly and the nature of fate.*

Matthews: The cautionary tale is a phrase I like. You can't, in fact, tell yourself how to be wiser and better. If you could, you would drive yourself nuts. I never liked it when other people did it for me. I suppose I would really hate it if I was the one telling *me* what was good for me. But the cautionary tale can remind you that your urge to control and to understand things is subject to all kinds of misfirings. Effects which are unintentionally comic or antic have a way of disrupting smoothness, disrupting placidity, requiring you to lose and recover your balance.

I don't think of the comic impulse in writing as being anything like relief or a range of tone. It actually embodies and imitates a kind of moral balance that we have all the time. It tells you that you are continually losing your sense of balance, certainty, and poise, and you need to recover it. We use jokes to deal with the subject matters that we find the most unsettling and most threatening to our poise—sex, death, etc. The comic impulse is deeply serious in poetry and particularly when it subverts the temptation to pontificate, to pull the soapbox out. Cautionary tales are often in a grim way quite funny. The situation in "Whiplash," for example, made writing about it all the more attractive to me. You might even say that the narrative impulse itself is comic. It may indicate an attempt to make a more credible consequence out of life than life actually ever provides us with. There is something hubristic and comic about the urge to tell stories. In fact, if poems included that comical caution against relying too much on storytelling, then I would be a lot happier. Of course, the Deep Image poem has very little room for the antic or the comic, and that was its other temperamental defect for me at the beginning.

Wojahn: *A notion of the cautionary tale has a lot of links to Freud, who has been one of your most abiding influences. Many of Freud's case studies read like a variety of fable.*

Matthews: They *are* fables in some way. "The Wolf Man" could be described as Aesop on acid. I think they are very beautiful as narratives, and they have a real symmetry because the kinds of behavior he is dealing with have coherence, but not a coherence that is immediately available. A series of disjunctions and comic misunderstandings are inevitable, and they are narratives without a lot of other parallels, although many of Kafka's paradoxical fables come to mind. Freud's writing on dreams and jokes and their relation to the unconscious were things that made absolute sense to me as I read them. I was about fourteen when I read that stuff. Of course, there was much that I didn't understand. I was too close to puberty to understand how complicated his model for the pull of the erotic was. I didn't understand, until the next time I went back to read his essays, that almost all his models of intellectual activity were transactional. Either money was changing hands or water was seeking a different level. I didn't understand how *active* they were as models, but I knew right away that the stuff about the dreams and the stuff about jokes was true because language was what I knew the most about.

Harms: *Peter Stitt described* Happy Childhood *as an attempt to unburden yourself of your passion and interest in Freud.*

Matthews: I never felt it a burden. I am one of the few admirers of Freud who has refused to be embarrassed by him. The lazy, wholesale bashing of Freud by usually not the brightest feminists seems to me disgraceful. We have to see him as a major writer before we ask how great a scientist and psychologist he was. He was a very important figure, a real pioneer. It's a fascinating life which he allows us to see, and he gives us much more of himself than almost any other public figure who is a

94

writer that I can think of, and with the least amount of defensiveness. Freud made all kinds of dumb moves and decisions and, by and large, was very candid about almost every one of them. He is the last person people should attack because he is the person quickest to doubt himself.

I think of *Happy Childhood* as a book about the need we have for stories, fables, explanations, and names, and the damage those needs do to us. And that comes from Freud, for he was such a student of stories, tales and myth. So I suppose Stitt is right in some sense. I felt that if I could write a book in which I could put some of that ambivalent need for *story* behind me, then Freud, who was such a tutelary figure for me, would appear in the poems less frequently after that. But Freud is too great of a figure for us lesser folks to shuck off. I happily await the time when, Freud's follies having been pointed out by all in this country, everybody again remembers what a great man he was.

Wojahn: *We could also talk about this notion of the cautionary tale as a form employed in your poems about jazz musicians, writers, and sports figures. They often focus on great artists who, because of age or addictions or some other sort of human failing, are in decline.* Time and Money *has a poem called "Babe Ruth Toward the End," and in an earlier poem about the aging Bud powell, you even give him a heroin habit that he didn't actually have.*

Matthews: Well, actually there is some debate about this. The guy who put together the very elaborately produced Bud Powell Verve set called Al Young and wanted to use a part of Al's poem in the liner notes. Al told him, "Oh, I have a friend who has a poem about Bud Powell, and you should use it." So the guy called me up and said, "Your poem is the best poem I've looked at for this anthology but I'm not going to use it— because Powell snorted heroin but never shot up." He was so *insistent* about this. It's like saying he never inhaled! It's technical virginity, and I don't believe it for a minute.

I saw Powell play several times, and once, between sets, Powell sat there staring at the wall. His back was to the room. The piano was against the wall, an upright. And his depression was so extraordinary that it seemed to be using up two-thirds of the oxygen in the room. I threw the heroin addiction into the poem because it seemed to me that he was more involved with heroin than people had said. So, given that it was a short poem, I thought it would be best not to have him just be depressed but to have him be in a more melodramatic state and trapped by himself. Imagine being Powell: when he was on, he was one of our four or five greatest jazz pianists. When you were on, you'd be great. You were enrapt, and your full attention was there. And then when you quit playing, you were just a depressed guy who couldn't manage his own life. I think all of my poems about artists are cautionary tales about the difference between . . . Put it this way: you are a writer when you have a pen in your hand, and the rest of the time you are just a biped. It is hard for us to remember that for some reason, which must be why I tell myself this story so frequently in poems.

Harms: *You do this a lot. You write about these sports figures and musical figures in ways that italicize the region where the tragedy in their lives and the consolation they receive from art is at its most present. Are you conscious of ennobling those figures as people who have achieved a kind of mastery that secures them but then traps them?*

Matthews: I do think it is a trap. Most biographies of artists, even the most reliable, empathetic, and well-researched ones, make you feel sometimes as though you're in [the] company of a monster. There are people for whom this is not true. When the huge Verdi biography came out about a year and half ago, I read through it and thought, "Well, I might rather go bowling with St. Paul, but this was no monster." I don't think that being an artist and taking your own pleasure and taking things seriously necessarily makes you a monster, but it has made huge numbers of people into monsters. Only a few of those people have had a talent large enough to be a compensation for what bastards they became. If large numbers of people are driven to low-grade monsterhood, and you want to act this way for the rest of your life, then you better damn well be on guard.

It's parallel to something I think about a lot at my age, which will be fifty-three next month. Most of the people older than I am in my department are bitter and unhappy. And I look at the remaining years that I may wind up teaching, and I think, there has got to be a way not to do this. What is it? In this way, in the poems that start with *Rising and Falling,* which began to include my sons and my domestic life much more than my earlier poems, there is an attempt to work out very direct and practical concerns. I probably have written more poems about musicians and composers and athletes in the last few years partly because this is a problem that becomes very apparent at the stage in life where I am now. And I think, there has got to be a way not to get caught in this bitterness. I, of course, don't know that there is. But it is a hell of a lot better to imagine that there is one and look for it than to just let it sweep over you like some kind of dreadful mental plague.

There are a lot of counter examples. I see Galway Kinnell here in the city, and he is gracious and generous, and his last book was his very best, better than *The Book of Nightmares,* I think. Gerry Stern, Phil Levine, Carolyn Kizer—I know a lot of poets who are pretty content, but I know a lot of poets in that age bracket who are grumpy and who could list off every prize they haven't won, and can't get through a conversation without chopping off two poets of about the same age and status. So that is where the cautionary tales come from. I don't imagine that I am immune to any of this stuff.

Harms: *Have your ambitions for poetry changed in the last few years? In your new book, in the poem "The Rookery at Hawthornden," you make some comments about what poetry can do. For instance, "The world's a poem we'll never learn to write" and "verse is easy and poetry is hard. / The brash choir, like a polyphonic heart, / beats loudly in the trees and does not ask / what poetry can do, infamous for making / nothing happen. The rooks and I rejoice / not to be mute." That seems to be saying something about why we make art and what the mission of art is.*

Matthews: Some of it is birdlike. The song is, "Here I am." And "Pleased to be conscious again." And I don't think that's a small thing. I do think that writing poetry imitates, in some ways, keeping alert, keeping your poise, keeping your curiosity, keeping all the balls up in the air. It's a model for an attentive life. If someone were to say, "What kind of symbolic actions, Mr. Burke, can a poem perform?" I would use images from juggling and images from choreography. It's about balance and

97

posture, in the largest sense of the words, poise in the largest sense of the word. These are some of the most important things that poetry teaches us. It also teaches us a certain ordinary bravery. It is good for the human spirit to speak the truth in public, in an unquivering voice. Writing imitates some of that. You especially forget all this after a long department meeting or in places where public speech happens and the rule seems to be not to speak or to speak as little of the truth as possible, and never to say what the real issues are.

I've always liked the phrase "symbolic action," although I don't think I mean anything close to what Kenneth Burke had in mind. Poetry does seem to imitate one's curiosity and one's moral alertness—one's generosity. It reasserts the power of laughter in the face of terrible things that one can do to people. I think it does a lot of things. Auden was wrong. It's not true that poetry makes nothing happen. But it tends to work its wonders in a very small arena. It makes you more interesting to yourself. And to you and me, at its best. It doesn't persuade anybody to reinstate the funds for the National Endowment for the Arts. But the power that it does have is very real. It has the power to perform a kind of cleansing or rinsing. Poetry has a necessary social component because language is social and historical. So that while these activities take place in solitude, there is a sense in which you are in company the whole time. The language represents the other people who aren't there physically. Poetry can actually do quite a lot.

Harms: *Another line in* Time and Money *suggests that poetry is trying to improve on "this babble that issues like a dial tone, from our bodies, / this empty talk that surrounds us and numbs us."*

Matthews: Our sense of that may be fairly recent in human history, the amount of babble, starting from the paper on the doorstep, which I am addicted to reading to start the day, or the television, which I don't think is the devil's instrument. Much of it is dull, but that is another problem. It's one reason why I have eschewed the fax machine, and that I'm still on the outer-net. I feel the world can get to me all too readily as it is. We need to be able to distinguish between meaningful noise and a merely electronic noise. People of the nomadic tribes sixteen centuries ago had nothing of this problem. They were hearing divine voices because there was not enough stimulation going on. Our overstimulation is a recent phenomenon—but a very real one. There is the danger that language can be debased by the sheer technological torrent of it.

Harms: *Do you see some of the more experimental movements in contemporary poetry, such as the Language writers, attempting to restore this "debased vernacular"?*

Matthews: Those are desperate voices. But I don't think the desperation these poets feel is illusory in any sense. It's not what I would do in the same situation, but I understand why they are taking measures that they see as extreme. Because extreme measures of one kind or another seem to be required.

Wojahn: *The issue of precision and truthfulness, even on the level of the word itself, is something that always strikes me as characteristic of your work—I'm thinking of your interest in puns and etymology and slipperiness of word meanings, such as "cleave" in your poem "Twins." This issue of definitions is something you've continually pointed out and something that you've continually exploited in your writing, just as Nabokov and Auden have. And both are figures you've elegized and have a lot of affection for. I have a feeling that, like Auden, the book you'd want to have with you on a desert island is a good dictionary.*

Matthews: Sure, the *O.E.D.* The big one. With a bookcase to hold all the volumes. If you could have a small library on a desert island, I would take all reference books. It's a sort of Borgesian conceit, this notion that all possible worlds and all possible books could be extracted from them, not that one person could do more than a tiny amount of that extraction; but you would be less lonely accompanied by those books than by anything else. At a certain point, the radical slipperiness of language becomes something not to be frustrated by, but to delight in. How hard it is to be absolutely unambiguous in English is suggested by the degree of torture which English is subjected to in a good legal contract or insurance policy. When the money is on the line and they really have to be unambiguous, they do terrible things to English in pursuit of their goal. It has been pointed out by a couple of friends and readers that I'm very fond of words like "slur," "mar," words in which one thing turns into another, in which lines are blurred. "Blur" would be another one of those. The slipperiness becomes a precaution against too great a reliance on precision and accuracy and too much hubris in being a wielder of the same. A poem in which a kind of Mexican stand-off can be achieved between the two is a poem I would find very satisfying to write.

Harms: *Because of the sorts of interests you have and because of the things that you write about and the way that you investigate your interest in language, there is an emphasis in your poetry on knowledge, facility, and wit. Critics are always characterizing you as a witty, smart poet. I think in this new book, you actually address that characterization.*

Matthews: I actually complain about that. Andrew Hudgins, in my personal favorite bit of blurb-ery, said that I was the most funny serious poet since Berryman. That is certainly a compliment. But it's also possible to say something like that in a way that suggests that I might be a delightful dinner companion. That seems to be a way to ignore, as I complain in *Time and Money,* that what goes into wit is the full measure of pain and rage and love that one brings to one's life. As I said earlier, there is nothing that is *relief* about the comic or the witty, as I understand it. I don't even particularly agree with the notion—fairly commonplace during the '60s when these short imagistic poems were highly praised by the prevailing taste—that irony is a defense against feeling. Irony is a form of feeling. Most of our feelings are deeply mixed. I think that the ironic and the antic and the comic get a kind of reflex low rating. And to mention it without the kind of rhetorical stress that Hudgins gave that little quote, in order to say, "Gee, I really mean this," does feel like faint praise. No one should expect praise, but if it is going to be offered, the faint praise isn't comparable to the other praise.

Wojahn: *What are your writing habits like? Do you write every day? Do you work from a notebook or diary?*

100

Matthews: No, I don't write every day. And I don't have a notebook or diary. I did keep them at one time. When you first start writing, so little of what you write is worth keeping in the form in which you write it. I would look at it, and I would think, well, maybe I could make something else out of this. And after a while, I realized that I had all of these little scraps of paper in a drawer somewhere and all I could do was *look* at them. There is the anecdote from which Donald Hall takes the title for one of his books. When he went back to the farm on which his grandparents had lived, he went through their effects after both of them had died. They were incredibly organized, and he found a box with a label on it that said, "string too short to be saved." And it was full of just such string. And I felt this way about the stuff in my drawer. I thought, "I don't know why I'm keeping this." Everyone's temperament is different, but for me, if I give that stuff away, the chance that it will come back in a usable form is much higher than if I keep it. So, for me, the superstition is that by not having a journal or notebook, I get rid of the loose ends that always, in a deceptive and sirenlike way, seem to say, "You can make something good of us." But the truth is that I didn't make anything good of them in the first place, and they need to be dead in their current form in order for any energy that is trapped in them to be released and maybe come back in a more usable or interesting form. For me, the superstition is that by not keeping a journal, I'm doing something good. Whether this is any more true than the opposite superstition, I have no idea.

About my not working every day: when my sons were small, I used to write in the evening because I was the only parent in the household for most of those years and I had heard so many bright women friends of mine feeling torn between wanting to get their work done and their domestic responsibilities. And I said, "Well, that's easy, I'll write at night." I was sort of an insomniac in those years anyway. But then they got older, and waiting for them to go to sleep meant that at a certain point I was starting to write at 11:30 at night. And that is going to be a cul de sac soon, you think. So I taught myself to write in the mornings, and then I just wrote when I could. I never understood how someone who has children could write at the same time every day, or even guarantee that you would get any writing done on a given day. It just didn't seem possible or sensible to plan. And Sebastian, my younger son, is thirty now. It has been a long time since they have been a part of the decision-making process about any of this stuff.

But I never wanted to do it differently. The first thing that happened when they weren't home was that I missed them terribly. I went through a serious empty-nest blues. My major reaction to their absence was, one, to miss them and, two, to realize how much of my own emotional life I had triflingly allowed to be shadowed by the pleasure I took in raising them. The ninth thing on the list was to think about how my writing habits might change. I wasn't sufficiently dissatisfied to change them. When I'm on a roll, I do work pretty much every day, and I find whatever time it is that I can do it. And I go through periods when it is like a pitcher letting his arm return to normal. You think, "I'm resting now." And that, too, is part of the process. If I don't write for a couple of weeks, I don't get anxious. There never fails to be a point that I am bored by rest and need to write. So I don't think of it as a menace or a block. It is just part of the way I do it.

Wojahn: *How do you go about revising a poem? How soon in the writing process do you figure you have a draft or how soon do you put it into the computer?*

Matthews: What computers have done to poets is an interesting question. I think poems are 20 percent longer than they used to be.

In revision, I do two things, and I do them simultaneously. One is to work towards getting a draft. I like to have a whole thing in front of me to be able to pick up and revise. But I also revise as I'm going along, which sounds like I'm less interested in getting to that whole thing and more interested in revising something that I don't even understand the full shape of yet. But both things happen simultaneously. Whether this is good or bad, I don't know. Then, when I have a draft, I put it on the computer because I like looking at it in type. My handwriting, if I'm working fast or if I'm getting excited, is something that only I can read. I like the objectification that a typeface gives the poem. I can look at it again and say to myself, "I wonder what I would do with this is if I had written it?" I pretend that I just found it, and that I have no idea where it came from, and that I am completely uninterested in the intentions and the confusions that I had the other day. I try to treat the poems as if they were newly discovered, as if they had been left there by a kind of reverse kleptomaniac. Before I had a PC, I used to type out the poems. Having the poem cast in typeface and not in my own handwriting helps me maintain the illusion that I didn't write it. What I really mean is that I'm supposed to be reminding myself not to be interested in the process that got me to that point, not to be loyal to any of it, and not to try to remember what I thought I was doing—because I don't care what those ideas were. All that is interesting is what is on the paper. I almost never do any actual composing on the computer. I basically use it for storage. For me, it's really just an extremely expensive typewriter and file cabinet, but I love it. I love not having to retype poems all the time. I like being able to write a letter and then change a few little things. I really find it a very companionable tool. But it sure is a lot of money for a typewriter with some storage space.

Harms: *Do you listen to music when you write?*

Matthews: If I listen to music, then I *can't* write. In my study, the desk is up against the wall. It would make a lot of sense to put it up against the window, but I've never done that. I want to be in an imaginary cell with the poem, though I like to think that I can get up from the cell and go to the part of the room where all my reference books are if I want to look something up. I've twice gone off to writer's colonies, but I don't particularly like them—I think of them as art jail. I really like working at home, where I'm near my reference books and can go to the kitchen to make coffee. Twice I've lived in places where there have been commanding views, and I moved my desk both times because I found myself just staring out the window.

Harms: *You've talked a lot in other interviews about jazz as an influence when you're writing—you've called it linguistic improvisation. How would you compare that to the sort of improvisation that we are familiar with in jazz?*

103

Matthews: Improvisation, as Mingus suggests, doesn't come out of nowhere. Think of all the things Gillespie and Parker and the pioneer boppers had to know—the chord changes to a couple hundred songs, for example. And think of the ability of opera singers to know hundreds of roles—Domingo must know 120 roles, and he can pretty much walk on stage and sing without a lot of research to remind him of what is going on. These are astonishing feats. I think that the real influence jazz has on poetry has to do with phrasing and timing, things easiest to talk about in relation to jazz singing, though the people I listened to most avidly as a kid were horn players. I listen very carefully to pianists these days, not that I've stopped listening to horn players or singers, but there are a lot of things I don't understand about how jazz piano works. So, I've listened to a lot of jazz piano lately, hoping to figure out what I can about it. What I've learned has something to do with variations on a melody that is never quite stated. Something even more important has to do with never coming in exactly on the beat. And it also has to do with how you move from one phrase to the next. I'm convinced that the best verse that I've written is not composed by the line but is composed by the phrase and the clause and the sentence. The line is a kind of necessary contradiction in the literal sense of the word, a counter-saying of what is actually going on. The line is an incredibly important unit, but it is not the unit of composition, though Alexander Pope would regard this as a ludicrous thing to say.

Wojahn: *But then you've got a lot of poems in* Time and Money *that are in strict form in ways that a lot of your earlier poems weren't—a lot of quatrains and a lot of sonnets.*

Matthews: The next book is going to have at least nineteen sonnets in it. I'm writing three series of six sonnets, and I'm going to have a lone wolf sonnet in it. And I don't know why. It's another one of those boredom issues. You just think, "I haven't written that many of these, and I'm really enjoying it, so I'll do it until I get tired of it." But I think particularly, the more compulsory the form is, if the form forces you to compose by the line and things get written and you can figure out a way to compose *through* the line, it is like the moment in early jazz when people start ignoring the bar sign at the end of the measure. So you stop getting that two-step um-pa rhythm effect, and you start getting stuff like the long breaks and pauses in the early Louis Armstrong Hot Five and Seven disks, where you think, "Now here is somebody who can hear his way all the way from the beginning of the solo to the end." And the first thing that has to happen to make this possible is for the bar sign to just go away. So, I don't know. If you push this metaphor too far and look for too many parallels, you start to talk nonsense. But there is some deep connection between poetry and music.

I'm particularly attracted to the sonnet for reasons I hadn't worried about until recently. I was thinking of the very early sonnets in English, and about how so many of them were poems of love and seduction. What you get in a sonnet is you have this incredibly rational structure which is applied to a body of psychic energy which is absolutely unamenable to the rational. The sonnet, like a particularly interesting and lively person, has this top layer of great sanity, structure, and rationalism—and a fanatic burbling of unconscious desires beneath that, some of which are unspeakable. The poise between the two in the sonnet is particularly interesting. Historically, the sonnet has always been susceptible to containing things in that way, and that's one reason why I like the form.

Harms: *So is it sort of an organic entity in some respect? Something that always amazes me about the writing of a sonnet is that the turn that takes place between octave and sestet just seems to happen. As if it were an organic aspect of the form.*

Matthews: As if you think at some point, "I've got to turn now." Or worse, or more eerily, as if *it* says, "I have got to turn now." It's particularly fun writing a series of sonnets in which none of the turns happen at the end of the eighth line. But the turn will happen. It's true, that if the model I just gave of the sonnet is not a purely fanciful one, something like the turn has to happen, so that power relationship between the two levels is potentially reversible. Otherwise, the sonnet stays too rationalized. There has to be a way for the steam to come up through the crust so you pierce the pastry dough.

Harms: *This is something I took from another interview where you were talking a lot about jazz: the paradoxical problem with the audience for both jazz and poetry is that both art forms have at their core a deep humanity, yet both are radically undervalued by the public. I was wondering about your understanding of audience, what kind of impact it has had on your work. There is so much talk in our discipline about what we can do about the problem of poetry's lack of audience.*

Matthews: I think Dana Gioia's ideas in his "Can Poetry Matter" essay, which got a lot of attention a few years ago, are basically a sort of commonsense attempt to transfer his marketing expertise in the business world to the world of poetry; yet the two fields are so different from one another that his plans can't help but fail. I don't know how the audience for poetry can be made larger. What worries me most about the poetry audience is not its size, which in fact seems to be growing. When Donald Hall's first book was published in 1956, it had a print run of five hundred copies, and it was an era of very few poetry readings. I think the audience for poetry has grown enormously in the last twenty years. But what worries me is that this audience is essentially a group of people who deliberately stand to the side of the social world, who wear their marginality as a badge. And furthermore, the notion that poetry should have a mass audience may be some American—or Russian—peculiarity. Large countries are subject to this dream, more than small countries, I think. I have never heard Norwegians complain about how few Norwegians read poetry. But you know, Maecenas was a reader, Augustus was a reader. Aside from Eugene McCarthy and Jimmy Carter (who are not quite of the same mettle, it seems to me), the worldly world doesn't care about poetry. Most people who care about poetry think of it as one of the badges of their unworldliness. They are members of a subsidized Bohemian class: teachers, students, grant applicants. They are off to the side. And it is understood that is where poetry happens. That seems to me a dangerous difference between the situations of Martial and Horace. Martial knew his audience was comparatively small. But if Martial and Horace did a good job of making fun of somebody important, they could get away with it. And they knew that the subject of their satire would hear about the poem and probably read it. But they also

106

knew that if they made fun of somebody important poorly, then there might be repercussions. Generally, that didn't happen, but Ovid did live out his last years on the Black Sea.

But it's the sense that poetry is proud to be off to the side that worries me. Obviously the idea that *everybody* in Shakespeare's time knew and loved poetry is just a sentimental idea. If we were to ask what percentage of the British population was literate, we would already know what was wrong with that model. The British and the French systems seek to screen out a small number of adolescents and educate the hell out of them and condemn everybody else to a life of working in a pharmacy. This model is impossible for Americans, for sentimental reasons, to agree with. And I think it is a cruel way to run a country. But our alternative, which is to educate everybody poorly, has not caused a widespread interest in poetry. I don't know the answer to this problem. To the extent that I ever think about an audience, I think of my reader as someone about my age, and that we share a wide range of cultural reference, so that I don't have to explain who the Five Satins were. And my reader is somebody [whom] I could be perfectly comfortable talking to, quite frankly, over a brandy or a glass of wine late at night. Beyond that, I never invest that person with any more of an identity or even a sex. This person is either a man or a woman or both. I don't personalize it any further than that. But I envision my reader as someone I could converse with, not read to.

Wojahn: *But don't you think that even the poets themselves have become more factionalized than ever? In the late '60s and '70s, when you were starting out, there seemed to be a kind of aesthetic catholicism. But today we have these tiny Balkanized camps of Language Poets who don't talk to formal poets and academic writers who don't talk to poetry slam aficionados. What do you make of the present scene?*

Matthews: I think it is a reflection of a general social malaise. I find that the English department in which I work is much more factionalized and politicized and territorial than it was in the '60s and '70s. I think society is more like this. In fact, very little melts in the melting pot. These sort of gummy accretions of like-minded people and special interest groups with the same special interests have a way of not getting mixed into the gruel that the melting pot ought to be producing. There is a failure of imagination at the social level, especially for a culture that is supposed to prize diversity. Everybody talks a big game about diversity, but what three-quarters of the people mean about diversity is, "I don't want the door shut until my group gets in." And it's a turf-war definition of diversity and not a genuinely catholic (with a small c) definition. It's easier to get elected. It's easier to get your research published. It's easier to do all kind of things by playing the "diversity card," to paraphrase Robert Shapiro's now-famous complaint, than to talk about what it is really like to have a culture in which different people can instruct each other on how life feels for them. I see very little true diversity in the culture at large. I think that in some sense poetry is following this trend toward fragmentation, though social punditry is not my forte. It does seem to me that the world is a somewhat shabbier place than it was when I was younger, and I don't know how much of that notion is pure sentimentalism and how much of it is true. But it seems to me that at one time there was a lot more discourse between poets of different inclinations and a sense that we were in on something big together. If we were all parasites on the same large wooly mammal, it was a good one. Rather than fight to see who got the most blood, we would cooperate to make sure that everybody could get a proboscis in the beast. It doesn't feel like that to me now. I won't name names. But I was recently at a poetry event where there were three or four people (these were all male poets—this happens among male poets more than among female poets, I think) about a generation below me, say fifteen years younger. I came into the room, and they were all standing in a clump, and they all turned and looked at me, and in each of their eyes was a clear look that I could easily translate. And it said, "When you die, can I have your toys?"

When I was younger, I needed older people to be around as much as possible because they knew a lot of stuff that I didn't. I don't remember being on the other end of such a frankly oedipal gaze. And there's another change I've noticed. It may well be that while poetry and fiction workshops cause no harm whatsoever (what harm does a bad poem or a bad story cause in the world?), people who like to beat up on workshops are really just lamenting the fact that they belong to a club that a lot of other people can get into, too. The motives are fairly transparent. One thing that may have happened as a result of the proliferation, or the distribution of the opportunity to try to be a writer to a wider number of people (which, after all, is a very American idea)—is that excellence will still be very elitist, but the opportunity will be absolutely equal. It is not that people are less generous than I was at their age, but they face a different demographic situation as artists. That would be my guess. And this may turn out to be the one serious problem with the proliferation of writing programs: it makes for a lot of unsatisfied people. But we also have to remember that people come to writing programs for a little dash of courage. They come to be around people who also write and care about it and don't think it's weird. They come to give each other courage and a certain kind of dignity that is hard to get elsewhere in the culture; they come to places and situations where it is bottled, as if it were compressed in a tank like gas. People must really need what they think they can get from such places.

Wojahn: *It sounds like you still take a lot of delight in teaching. Many teachers, of writing or anything else, don't necessarily retain that energy by the time they reach their 40s and 50s.*

Matthews: Yeah, I'm lucky. I still enjoy teaching a lot. My patience for almost everything else that goes on in academic life has plummeted. I have had to work hard not to be fliply cynical. I spend more calories guarding against that than I used to, I notice. I hope that is not going to be a problem in the next chunk of life ahead of me. I certainly worry about it. But the actual teaching is fine. There have been a couple of times in my career when I haven't enjoyed teaching because I felt I was struggling against the grain of the assignment I had been given and I had been asked to do something that I didn't really have the experience or the wherewithal to do. And at that point, you feel yourself flounder and hate it. For better or for worse, I've become a kind of specialist and pretty much now teach only what I'm good at. While there are some dangers in that, it saves you from that other business. Everybody has been given a couple of courses like that somewhere along the line, and it is very painful to slog your way through them while knowing what a mediocre job you're doing. Those were the times when I've thought it would be easy to dislike life as a teacher under the right or, in this case, the wrong circumstances. The stuff that can wear you down are issues of daily civility and governance in the department life, and when those things grow too complicated, you have to work very hard to seal off the actual teaching from everything else. As the money and morale get lower and lower in the well around the country, and especially around the education community (and it is going to continue in this way for the next several years), I think we are all going to spend more time and more calories sealing off the classroom in that way, from the rest of it, which is going to cause a lot of steady and low grade discomfort. I hope I'm wrong.

Harms: *Have you noticed a change over the years in your student writers' relationship to what they are doing? Have they changed?*

Matthews: The last one first: have they changed? Yes. When I started teaching, they were 75 percent male. They are now 75 percent female, and that's a major change, the effects of which we have only begun to understand. Another change is something you touched on when you spoke of a certain professionalization of writing programs. I think this can be a problem. It's less of a problem for me because the average age of my own students is probably thirty five. I don't have a single student who if you said to him or her, "what do you do?" would reply, " I'm a graduate student." They all have another professional or familial identity. They are very serious as writers, and the best of them are quite skillful. I think there are slightly more Hispanic and Afro-American writers in workshops than there used to be. This doesn't always make the terms of the debate any richer. For example, the better black students that I have had at City College tend to have a very different set of assumptions about their relationship to an audience and to a tradition and to a community than the white students, who have no idea [whom] they are speaking for and to, and don't think this is a problem. And the white and black students often clash, rather affectionately. The animus is not at all racial, or cultural even. But there is a real difference in the understanding of what it means to be a poet and what it means to speak as if you have an audience. Or, in the case of the white students, to speak as if you didn't know you had an audience and need to find out why you were speaking anyway. Sometimes that can be an issue. (I wouldn't say it needs to be divisive.) I think both parties actually learn something from it, and we figure out how to have a common vocabulary, and we go on, and people from both camps do good work, and they seem less like members of camps. All the good things that should happen, happen if the workshop is well run and if the students are basically generous and honest. But at the beginning, there is a real moment where people have to stop and figure out that they are not speaking the same language, and what does this mean?

I think the biggest problem is that they have no preparation, or what we think of as preparation. Maybe they have something that does prepare them, and we just don't recognize it because we are old fogies, but my sense is that the academic turf wars have destroyed the canon: there are some things that are good about that and some things that are very bad about it. One of the bad things is that it's very difficult to figure out what your graduate students have read. The texts everybody in your class has read are very small in number. It used to be that you could wrestle a liberal education out of an undergraduate institution, patching it together with the various things you were curious about, and then you went to graduate school and you did some more reading there. By the end of graduate school, you had a list of things you wanted to go back and read or things you never got to. If you were an active student, you could give yourself a "literary" education if you were trying to become a literary person, but now no institution offers anything remotely like that. I visit campuses where I run into students who have never opened the *Greek Anthology* and can't name more than nine of Shakespeare's plays. This is scandalous, and it seems to me the biggest problem that these kids face. In fact, no one was giving a liberal education to people who might want to become writers. Turning someone into a writer is not the job of a liberal education: writing is much too specialized. But, at one time, you could pick and choose; an undergraduate could put together a liberal education on a roll-your-own basis. Today it's very hard for students to arrange to have anything remotely like that. Surely, they don't like having someone like me telling them that they are unprepared. And I don't. It's not acceptable discourse to say to people, "You should have had horses," when no horses were available.

Wojahn: *Your* Selected Poems *doesn't include a lot of poems from your individual selections that I might have expected you to include, and it also emphasized a lot of your "sideline" work—the translations, the one-liner poems, as well as some uncollected poems. How did you hit upon the structure you employed in selecting the poems?*

Matthews: This is partly an attempt to convert commercial considerations into artistic opportunity. Peter Davison, my editor, wanted me to compile a *New and Selected*. And my sense is that the new poems in a *New and Selected* get lost; they don't get read with the same curiosity or in the same richness of context that they'd have if they were in a book by themselves. I thought, maybe a little melodramatically, "What can I offer him that will relieve me of the need to bury some new poems in a *New and Selected?*" The material that is "sideline-ish" in nature is often stuff I am especially fond of. I actually thought of the selected as more of a chance to rescue stuff from being out of print than as a way of representing myself, whom I hardly know in that way. To be asked to have a historical perspective on yourself as a writer is an impossible and perhaps a dangerous task. There is a longish uncollected poem in there called the "Waste Carpet," which is a poem I've always liked. It's for the most part unrevised. My superstition is that that's as it should be. Rather than gussying up your old work, you should be writing new poems. However, I liked that poem so much that I revised the last quarter of it. Not heavily, but significantly. The small changes I made seemed to have made a lot of difference, or so it seemed, probably because I have always liked the poem and felt that I hadn't quite got it right. Other than that, I basically thought, "This is work I don't want to see go into oblivion before its time, and I have been given the opportunity to rescue some of it." I had a slight tendency to prefer poems that I thought were underloved and underanthologized—poems that I seemed to have liked more than others did. I thought I would give the world a second chance to fall in love with them. I didn't treat the book as a knowledgeable self-portrait of myself as a writer. I thought, "What can I resuscitate?" Now that the warehousing costs have become the major financial issue for publishers, things don't stay in print as long as they used to. It seems to me that some of my poems may need the second chance that a *Selected Poems* presents.

Harms: *Tell me more about the book that you are writing now: are you thinking ahead about where you want your poetry to go?*

Matthews: I never think in those terms: I've always simply found the next thing to do. And I've always trusted that process without thinking too much about it. I am going to do more translation. After the Follain book, I didn't do much translation until I began the Martial book, which is now just out. I am two-thirds of the way through with a translation of Horace's satires. Horace is more challenging than Martial, if only because of the length of the poems: only a couple of the satires are shorter than a hundred lines. I've also accepted an invitation to do something for a new series of verse translations of the Greek tragedies, which University of Pennsylvania Press is planning. I'm going to do *Prometheus Bound*. My opportunities to do translations are arriving either by my own device or by somebody else's. And I find that I welcome them whenever they show up. And I like working on two things at once, although my answer to your question may suggest why I don't have longer-range plans than I do.

The current book has its title stolen from a Scott Joplin rag—*Strenuous Life*, it's called. In the last three years or so, my father died, and my wife got a cancer that she was first told was fatal. Then it was rediagnosed, and it was a very aggressive tumor, and it took a year of constant chemotherapy and radiation. At the end of that time, when the treatment was over and the first diagnostic tests, MRIs, etc., were taken, and the possibility that the tumor was entirely gone (that this incredibly aggressive tumor had been repelled by an incredibly wearing and aggressive treatment), her mother died. And she went to Rochester to do the kind of stuff you do in the wake of a parent's death, and has stayed in Rochester ever since, in very good health but absolutely unwilling to come back to New York, which in some way she associates with her illness. I've been under siege for three years in some way, which I take as an opportunity not to treat myself like a fort.

But all of this led me to think about writing a book such as a title like *Strenuous Life* suggests. It's about the degree to which life requires tremendous exertion, and I wanted to include a series of poems which were all written in the gravitational pull of that idea—somewhat in the way that *Happy Childhood* is caught in the gravitational pull of its concerns or the looser concerns of *Foreseeable Futures*, which is, ironically, a book about our obsession with our pasts. My job right now is to finish *Strenuous Life*, which is about unusual strenuousnesses, on the one hand. There is a poem or two that I'm going to write for it which are about a subject that I've never written about before but one so obvious I can't ignore it: I have had, for years, various durable but endurable orthopedic problems. The truth of the matter is that for most of my adult life, I have been in bearable but steady pain, a situation which I think a lot of people have been in. There is a dull roar from the pain at all times. I want to write a little bit about physiology and pain and managing pain and ignoring and living with it and so forth. So, the title has started to pull in all sorts of possibilities, to remind me what I might have paid more explicit attention to, but didn't. "Who wants to hear himself complain?" is what you first think; but on the other hand, you think, "But wait a minute. I actually think about this, and I have feelings about this." Just because it's not polite to stop strangers on the street and talk to them about your physical pain doesn't mean that you shouldn't be writing about it. What's always happened to me with my writing is that some set of fairly practical concerns and curiosities [has] suggested an enterprise that I try to shape into a book, a somewhat focused curiosity. I have no idea what the next one will be, but they don't stop. My assumption is that they will come along. I've never thought that it would be a good thing or a bad thing to write a long poem, for example, which might be one of the answers to the question, "What do you foresee?" I mean, I've never wanted to do it, but it doesn't mean that it wouldn't happen.

I'm going to translate Horace's *Epodes* when I get done with his satires. And I'm sort of interested in translating Ovid's *Amores*, not the *Ars Amoratia*, but the *Amores*, the slangier, more discursive, less didactic, more dramatic poems, which I think are more interesting than the *Art of Love*, and which have not been particularly well translated. It's funny that the Roman poets have been so poorly served by translators. Martial's been given the best attention, but in the case of Horace, for example, Pope translated only a few of the *Satires*, and just a few of the *Epistles*. After that the translators have been mostly classicists with indifferent skills as versifiers. There is a large body of that work that has not received any good, serious attention.

Harms: *It sounds as if when you're translating, you're writing as well.*

Matthews: Yes, I'm usually writing as well. In fact, I just went on a little spree. Until about ten days ago, I was writing extremely well and extremely fast and dropped the Horace completely, and I haven't touched it for about six weeks. But in the last week or so, I've been doing nothing. And I've been quite content. Now I'm starting to itch again. I may well start by doing a Horace satire or two, and then I'll go back to the book that I'm working on. But I often alternate and sometimes work on both projects in the same day.

Wojahn: *When you translate, do you do a literal translation first? Do you consult other translations?*

Matthews: I consult other translations, and, in the case of the Martial, I had a stack of about five Martial translations. He's been well-served; Dudley Fitts did a translation that was pretty good. And Rolfe Humphries did a translation. There is also one by James Michie, the Scots poet, which I don't like quite as well as the other two, but which in a few places is very good. And then there are various other translations. The person who I think would have been perfect for Martial at one stage of his writing life is J. V. Cunningham, who did two or three versions that are perfect. But that was it. So I used all of those. I have some other translations, none of which I particularly like. But they are all done by classicists, who are better Latinists than I am. So I'll look at the Latin, and then I'll look at their translations, and I'll say, "Oh, I see why he did that. That is an unusual ablative construction, and he is so much of a classicist that he is trying to preserve that, but the way you actually do that in English is. . . ." So there is plenty to be learned from them, even if the verse translation is not what I think it ought to be. I have looked up a lot of the historical background material, and I'm now pretty informed; I could go on a quiz show and do fine. But I don't know everything that somebody who studied Latin literature all his life does, and occasionally their footnotes are very helpful—the kind of stuff you need to know that goes beyond mythology or identifying the various emperors. In the Roman courts, for example—this is when people were still outside, before they had actually entered the court room—everyone is in the forum scuffing up the dirt and the stones, and somebody from the court comes out and says, "We believe that so and so is the defendant in this suit. Can you identify him?" And if you can, you signify by turning your head so that they can touch your ear lobe. And there is a famous passage in Horace that I never figured out in which somebody touches an ear-lobe. I needed to run across somebody whose knowledge of Roman legal practice was good enough so that he could tell me what was going on. Instances like these are when you are really grateful for the experts, even though their translations may not be too zippy.

Harms: *It seems like you have a lot to do.*

Matthews: It's work that I have been reading since I was a boy. It's like when I first read Stevens when I was younger. I thought, "When I am old enough, which I am not yet, I am going to do this." And I didn't have any specific program for what I had to do to be old enough, but I just knew that I wasn't quite up to it yet. I had always thought that I would do at least Martial and that, if the Martial went well, then I would take a deep breath and do Horace. And if I could do Horace, I could surely do the *Amores,* which are not as complicated technically or intellectually. Horace is as good as Virgil. He just doesn't like writing about people who aren't alive! Of course, Virgil doesn't write about anybody who isn't either a god or a fictional character.

Harms: *One last question: did you feel that something significant happened when your* Selected Poems *came out?*

Matthews: A *Selected* offers readers a chance to look at your work chronologically, for whatever narrative that implies. After all, there are few readers who have been with you the whole time. As with my earlier anecdote about the three oedipal younger poets, it makes you aware that you are passing into a different stage in the eyes of the world. It doesn't make me feel particularly different, but the poetry world is invited to look at you in slightly different ways, some of which would normally occur with the passage of time. But others wouldn't be noticed unless there were milestones—like a *Selected*. I think of it as one of the seven warning signs of being fifty for a poet!

Editors

Kurt Brown is the author of three full-length collections of poetry: *Return of the Prodigals* (Four Way Books, 1999), *More Things in Heaven and Earth* (Four Way Books, 2002), and *Fables from the Ark* (CustomWords, 2004). A fourth collection, *Future Ship*, is due out from Story Line Press in 2005. The editor of six anthologies of poetry and essays, he teaches creative writing at Sarah Lawrence College in Bronxville, New York.

Meg Kearney's book of poetry, *An Unkindness of Ravens,* was published by BOA Editions in 2001. Her collections of poems for teens, *The Secret of Me,* will be published in 2005. She has been featured on *Poetry Daily,* and her work has appeared or is forthcoming in numerous publications, including *Agni, Ploughshares,* and *Poetry,* and the anthologies *Where Icarus Falls, Urban Nature, The Poets' Grimm: 20th Century Poems from Grimm Fairy Tales, Shade,* and *The Book of Irish American Poetry from the 18th Century to the Present.* Recipient of an Artist's Fellowship in 2001 from the New York Foundation for the Arts, she received a *New York Times* Fellowship and the Alice M. Sellers Academy of American Poets Award in 1998. She has taught poetry at The New School University, and was associate director of the National Book Foundation for more than 10 years. She is now director of the Solstice Creative Writing Programs of Pine Manor College in Chestnut Hill, Mass.

Donna Reis's nonfiction book, *Seeking Ghosts in the Warwick Valley,* was published by Schiffer Publishing Limited in 2003. She received her M.A. in creative writing from the City College, City University of New York, where she studied with William Matthews. Her poetry, articles, essays, and criticisms have appeared in numerous magazines, including *The American Book Review, A Gathering of the Tribes, Cumberland Poetry Review, Hudson Valley Magazine,* and *Hanging Loose.* She received the Meyer Cohn Essay Award in Literature in 2000 and the James Ruoff Memorial Essay Award in 2002 from The City College of New York.

Estha Weiner's poems have appeared or are forthcoming in the anthologies *Never Before: Poems About First Experiences* (Four Way Books, 2005), *The Poets' Grimm: 20th Century Poems from Grimm Fairy Tales* (Story Line Press, 2003), and *Summer Shade: A Collection of Modern Poetry* (Wyndham Hall Press, 2001), and in such publications as *The New Republic, Barrow Street, Rattapallax, Brilliant Corners,* and *Lit.* A finalist for "Discovery"/ *The Nation* Prize, she is founder and director of the Writers' Night Series for Sarah Lawrence College and a Speaker on Shakespeare for the New York Council for the Humanities. WNET, Public Television, has recently made her a consultant.

Contributors

Cynthia Atkins's poems have been published in *American Letters & Commentary, Bomb, Bloomsbury Review, Chelsea, Denver Quarterly, Seattle Review, Seneca Review, Tar River Poetry, The Texas Review,* and *Verse.* She is currently visiting assistant professor of English at Sweetbriar College.

Coleman Barks is best known for his Rumi translations, *The Essential Rumi* (Harper, 1997) and *The Book of Love* (Harper, 2003), but he also publishes his own poetry, most recently *Tentmaking* (Maypop, 2001) and *Club: Granddaughter Poems* (Maypop, 2002). His newest translation is *The Drowned Book* (Harper Collins, 2004), the lost notebooks of Rumi's earthy and ecstatic father, Bahauddin.

Judith Baumel is the author of *The Weight of Numbers* (Wesleyan University Press, 1988) and *Now* (Miami University Press, 1996). She lives in New York City.

Jeanne Marie Beaumont's first book, *Placebo Effects* (Norton, 1997), was selected by William Matthews for the National Poetry Series. *Curious Conduct* was published by BOA Editions in 2004. She also coedited *The Poets' Grimm: 20th Century Poems from Grimm Fairy Tales* (Story Line Press, 2003)

Marvin Bell's latest books are *Nightworks: Poems 1962–2000* (Copper Canyon, 2003) and *Rampant* (Copper Canyon, 2004). His work includes what are known as the "Dead Man" and "Dead Man Resurrected" poems. Besides teaching for the University of Iowa, he leads an annual workshop for America SCORES teachers, teaches a master class for the Rainier Writing Workshop M.F.A. at Pacific Lutheran University in Tacoma, and serves as the state of Iowa's first poet laureate.

Earl. S. Braggs, a North Carolina native, is the author of five books of poetry including his latest, *Crossing Tecumseh Street* (Anhinga Press, 2003). Currently, Braggs teaches at the University of Tennessee at Chattanooga, where he is a UC Foundation Professor of English.

Andrea Carter Brown's first collection, *Brook & Rainbow*, won the Sow's Ear Press Chapbook Competition in 2001. *The Disheveled Bed*, her first full-length collection, is forthcoming from CavanKerry Press. Her work has won awards from the Poetry Society of America, the *Writer's Voice, The River Oak Review, Thin Air,* and *The MacGuffin.* Her magazine publications include *Gettysburg*

Review, Mississippi Review, Ploughshares, and *Five Points.* She studied with William Matthews in the graduate creative writing program at CCNY.

Harriet Brown's poems have appeared in *Poetry, Prairie Schooner, Southern Poetry Review,* and other literary magazines. Her chapbook, *The Promised Land,* was published in 2004 by Parallel Press. She is the author of *The Goodbye Window* (University of Wisconsin Press, 1998) and other nonfiction books. She lives in Madison, Wisconsin.

Robert Burr lives in Hunter's Point, New York, and currently teaches English composition at the City College, City University of New York, and is a friend of Poets House in New York city.

Mark Cox teaches in the Department of Creative Writing at University of North Carolina-Wilmington. His honors include a Whiting Writers Award, a Pushcart Prize, the Oklahoma Book Award, and The Society of Midland Authors Poetry Prize. He has served as poet in residence at The Frost Place in Franconia, New Hampshire. His latest books are *Thirty Seven Years from the Stone* (Pitt Poetry Series, 1998), and *Natural Causes* (University of Pittsburgh Press, 2004).

Stephen Cramer's book, *Shiva's Drum,* was selected by Grace Schulman for the National Poetry Series competition and will be published by University of Illinois Press in 2004. His work has appeared in journals such as *Atlanta Review, Quarterly West,* and *Mid-American Review.* He lives with his wife, Joanna, in New York City.

Sascha Feinstein won the 1999 Hayden Carruth Award for his poetry collection, *Misterioso* (Copper Canyon, 2000). His work has appeared in *American Poetry Review, The Penguin Book of the Sonnet, The New Grove Dictionary of Jazz,* and elsewhere. He chairs the English department at Lycoming College and edits *Brilliant Corners: A Journal of Jazz & Literature.*

Allen C. Fischer brings to poetry a background in business, where he was a director of marketing. He says Bill Matthews jump-started his writing and offered guidance for fifteen years. Fischer's poems have appeared in *Indiana Review, Poetry, Prairie Schooner,* and *Rattallapax.*

Debra Fried studied at Purchase College and at the City College of New York, where she was briefly a student of William Matthews.

Rachel Hadas is Board of Governors Professor of English at Rutgers University, where she has taught for more than two decades at the Newark campus. She is the author of more than a dozen books of poetry, criticism, and translations. Her latest collection is *Laws* (Zoo Press, 2004).

Daniel Halpern is the author of nine collections of poetry, most recently *Something Shining* (Knopf, 1999), *Selected Poems* (Knopf, 1994), and *Foreign Neon* (Knopf, 1991). He is editor of *The Art of the Tale* and *The Art of the Story*, and for twenty five years edited *Antaeus*. He is currently Editorial Director of Ecco, an imprint of HarperCollins and lives in Princeton, New Jersey, with his wife, the writer Jeanne Wilmot, and their daughter, Lily.

James Harms is the author of four books of poetry, including *Freeways and Aqueducts* (Carnegie Mellon University Press, 2004). He directs the creative writing program at West Virginia University.

Pamela Harrison worked with William Matthews at the Catskill Poetry Workshop and in 2002 was named PEN Northern New England Discovery Poet. Her book of poems is *Stereopticon* (David Robert Books, 2004). She lives in Vermont.

Walter R. Holland lives in New York and is the author of two books of poetry, *A Journal of the Plague Year: Poems 1979–1992* (Magic City Press, 1992) and *Transatlantic* (Painted Leaf Press, 2001), and a novel, *The March* (Masquerade Books, 1996). He holds a Ph.D. in English from the City University of New York and currently teaches poetry and literature at the New School University as well as being a physical therapist.

Ann Hurwitz studied with William Matthews for about four years at City College. She teaches at Bank Street College, a graduate school of education.

Richard Jackson's most recent books are *Unauthorized Autobiography: New and Selected Poems* (Ashland University Press, 2003) and *Heartwall* (University of Massachusetts Press, 2000). He has won Guggenheim, Fulbright, National Endownment for the Arts, National Endownment for the Humanities, and Witter Bynner Fellowships, and five Pushcart Prize selections. He edits *Poetry Miscellany*, and is the author of two award-winning critical books.

Jacqueline Johnson is a multidisciplined writer working in the areas of poetry, books for children, fiction, and nonfiction. She is the winner of the Third Annual White Pine Press Award in 1997 for her collection of poems, *A Gathering of Mother Tongues* (White Pine Press, 1998). She is at work on a new book, *The Place Where Memory Dwells*.

Rodney Jones is the author of six books of poetry: *The Story They Told Us of Light* (Alabama, 1980), *The Unborn* (Atlantic Monthly, 1985), *Transparent Gestures* (Houghton Mifflin, 1989), *Apocalyptic Narrative* (Houghton Mifflin, 1993), *Things That Happen Once* (Houghton Mifflin, 1996), *Elegy for the Southern Drawl* (Houghton Mifflin, 1999) and *The Kingdom of the Instant* (Houghton Mifflin,

2002). His honors include a Guggenheim Fellowship, the Lavan Award of the American Academy of Arts and Letters, the Jean Stein Award of the American Academy and Institute of Arts and Letters, and the 1989 National Book Critics Circle Award.

Meg Kearney's book of poetry, *An Unkindness of Ravens,* was published by BOA Editions in 2001. Her collections of poems for teens, *The Secret of Me,* will be published in 2005. She has been featured on *Poetry Daily,* and her work has appeared or is forthcoming in numerous publications, including *Agni, Ploughshares,* and *Poetry,* and the anthologies *Where Icarus Falls, Urban Nature, The Poets' Grimm: 20th Century Poems from Grimm Fairy Tales, Shade,* and *The Book of Irish American Poetry from the 18th Century to the Present.* Recipient of an Artist's Fellowship in 2001 from the New York Foundation for the Arts, she received a *New York Times* Fellowship and the Alice M. Sellers Academy of American Poets Award in 1998. She has taught poetry at The New School University, and was associate director of the National Book Foundation for more than 10 years. She is now director of the Solstice Creative Writing Programs of Pine Manor College in Chestnut Hill, Mass.

David Keller's most recent collection is *Trouble in History* (White Pine Press, 2000). He first met Bill Matthews in 1981, at The Frost Place in Franconia, New Hampshire, and they became friends. Mr. Keller has served as director of admissions for the annual Frost Place Festival of Poetry for many years.

Gerry LaFemina is the author of several collections of poetry, including *Shattered Hours: Poems 1988–1994, Zarathustra in Love* (Mayapple Press, 2001), *Graffiti Heart* (winner of the Anthony Piccione/MAMMOTH Books Poetry Prize, 2001), and *The Window Facing Winter* (New Issues Poetry and Prose, 2004). He has taught at West Virginia University, Sarah Lawrence College, and Grand Valley State University, among other schools.

Peter Makuck is Distinguished Professor of Arts and Sciences at East Carolina University, and has published five collections of poetry, a collection of short stories, and a book of essays on the Welsh poet Leslie Norris. The recipient of the 1993 Charity Randall Citation from the International Poetry Forum and editor of *Tar River Poetry,* he lives in Pine Knoll Shores, North Carolina.

Gary Margolis is the Director of the Center for Counseling and Human Relations at Middlebury College. He has been a Frost Fellow and staff member at the Bread Loaf Writers' Conference. His new book of poems is *Fire in the Orchard* (Autumn House Press, 2002).

Cleopatra Mathis has published five books of poetry, most recently *What to Tip the Boatman?* (Sheep Meadow Press, 2003). Her work has been widely published in anthologies, textbooks, magazines, and journals, including: *The New Yorker, Triquarterly, American Poetry Review, The Extraordinary Tide, New Poetry By American Women,* and *The Made Thing: An Anthology of Southern Poetry.* She teaches at Dartmouth College.

Sebastian Matthews is the son of William Matthews. He is a writer, poet, and teacher at Warren Wilson College and is the editor of a new literary journal, *Rivendell.* He has published a memoir of his father, *In My Father's Footsteps* (W. W. Norton, 2003). He lives in Asheville, North Carolina.

Karen McCosker lives in northern Maine, where she is lecturer in language arts at the University of Maine at Presque Isle. Her poems have been published in *Harvard Review, Wisconsin Review, Many Mountains Moving, The South Carolina Review,* and online in *Isle Review.* She is the editor of the anthology *A Poem a Day* (Steerforth Press, 1996)

Christopher Merrill's books of prose include *Only the Nails Remain: Scenes from the Balkan Wars* (Rowan & Littlefield, 1999). He is also the author of four poetry collections: *Workbook* (Teal Press, 1988), *Fevers and Tides* (Teal Press, 1989), *Watch Fire* (White Pine Press, 1994), and *Brilliant Water* (White Pine Press, 2001). He directs the International Writing Program at the University of Iowa.

Judson Mitcham has published two collections of poems, *Somewhere in Ecclesiastes* (University of Missouri Press, 1991) and *This April Day* (Anhinga, 2003), as well as two novels, *The Sweet Everlasting* (1996) and *Sabbath Creek* (2004), both from the University of Georgia Press. He teaches psychology at Fort Valley State University.

Robert Morgan's first collection, *Zirconia Poems,* was published by William Matthews and Russell Banks at Lillabulero Press in 1969. Since then, he has won many awards and published essays, short stories, and novels, as well as more books of poetry, including *At the Edge of the Orchard Country* (Wesleyan University Press, 1987), *Green River: New and Selected Poems* (Wesleyan University Press, 1991), and *Topsoil Road* (Louisiana University Press, 2000). He is Kappa Alpha Professor of English at Cornell.

Sharon Olds is an award-winning poet and author of many books, including *Satan Says* (University of Pittsburgh Press, 1980), *The Dead and the Living* (Random House, 1984), *The Gold Cell* (Knopf, 1987), *The Father* (Random House, 1992), *The Wellspring* (Knopf, 1996), *Blood, Tin, Straw* (Knopf, 1999), and *The Unswept Room* (Knopf, 2002). She teaches in the creative writing program at New York University.

Rick Pernod is the director of Exoterica, a literary organization that produces the Exoterica Reading Series, WORD: The Jay Liveson Memorial Poetry & Music Festival, and administers the National Arts Club/Con Edison High School Essay Writing Scholarship. He is a creative writing instructor at City College in New York and recently has had work translated into Spanish and featured in the Nicaraguan journal *400 Elephants*. He studied under Bill Matthews at CCNY as a graduate student.

Stanley Plumly is the author of many collections of poetry, including *The Marriage in the Trees* (Ecco Press, 1997), *Boy on the Step* (Ecco Press, 1989), *Summer Celestial* (Ecco Press, 1983) and *Out of the Body Travel* (W. W. Norton, 1977). He has edited the *Ohio Review* and the *Iowa Review*. He is a professor of English at the University of Maryland, College Park.

Donna Reis's nonfiction book, *Seeking Ghosts in the Warwick Valley*, was published by Schiffer Publishing Limited in 2003. She received her M.A. in creative writing from the City College, City University of New York, where she studied with William Matthews. Her poetry, articles, essays, and criticisms have appeared in numerous magazines, including *The American Book Review, A Gathering of the Tribes, Cumberland Poetry Review, Hudson Valley Magazine,* and *Hanging Loose*. She received the Meyer Cohn Essay Award in Literature in 2000 and the James Ruoff Memorial Essay Award in 2002 from The City College of New York.

Kenneth Rosen founded the Stonecoast Writers' Conference in 1980 at the Gorham Campus of the University of Southern Maine, where he teaches. His many books include *The Hebrew Lion* (1989), *Longfellow Square* (1991), and *No Snake, No Paradise* (1996), all from Ascensius Press.

Vern Rutsala is the author of many volumes of poetry. His tenth collection, *A Handbook for Writers: New and Selected Poems* was published by White Pine Press in 2004. Recent work has appeared in *Poetry, Mississippi Review,* and *North American Review*. The 2004 winner of the Akron Poetry Prize, his latest book, *How We Spent Our Time,* is forthcoming in 2005 from the University of Akron Press.

John Schenck was born in Mt. Kisco, New York, and graduated from Yale University with a B.A. in English in 1965. A classmate of Bill Matthews, he was also a student in Bill's poetry workshop at CUNY in 1997.

Dave Smith is the Elliot Coleman Professor of Poetry at Johns Hopkins University. From 1990 through 2003, he was the coeditor of *The Southern Review* at Louisiana State University. His most recent books include *The Wick of Memory:*

New and Selected Poems 1970–2000 (Louisiana State University Press, 2000) and *Floating on Solitude: Three Books of Poems* (University of Illinois Press, 1997).

Henry Taylor is professor of literature and codirector of the M.F.A. Program in creative writing at American University in Washington, D.C. His third collection of poems, *The Flying Change* (Louisiana State University Press, 1986), received the Pulitzer Prize; his first two books, *The Horse Show at Midnight* (Louisiana State University Press, 1966) and *An Afternoon of Pocket Billiards* (University of Utah Press, 1975), were reissued in one volume by Louisiana State University Press in 1992.

Melinda Thomsen teaches English/English as a second language at LaGuardia Community College in New York. Her poetry has been published in several literary magazines, including *Rattle* and *Main Street Rag*. She received her M.A. in English/creative writing from the City College, CUNY.

Richard Tillinghast is the author of seven books of poetry as well as *Damaged Grandeur*, a critical memoir of the poet Robert Lowell (University of Michigan Press, 1995). His most recent poetry collection is *Six Mile Mountain* (Story Line Press, 2000). A faculty member in the Master of Fine Arts program at the University of Michigan, he is also a director of The Poets House in Ireland.

Sidney Wade has published four collections of poems, most recently *Celestial Bodies* (Louisiana State University Press, 2002). She has also published *Green* (University of South Carolina Press, 1998), *From Istanbul/Istanbul'dan* (poems in translation, English/Turkish, Yapi Kredi Yayinlari, Istanbul, 1998), and *Empty Sleeves* (University of Georgia Press, 1991). She has taught at the University of Florida in the creative writing program since 1993.

Bruce Weigl is the author of more than a dozen books of poetry, including *Song of Napalm* (Atlantic, 1991), *Sweet Lorain* (Triquarterly, 1996), *Archeology of the Circle: New and Selected Poems* (Grove, 1999), and most recently *The Unraveling Strangeness* (Grove, 2002). He has edited or coedited three collections of critical essays and has translated from the Vietnamese, Romanian, and Spanish. In 2000, Grove published his memoir *The Circle of Hanh*.

Estha Weiner's poems have appeared or are forthcoming in the anthologies *Never Before: Poems About First Experiences* (Four Way Books, 2005), *The Poets' Grimm: 20th Century Poems from Grimm Fairy Tales* (Story Line Press, 2003) and *Summer Shade: A Collection of Modern Poetry* (Wyndham Hall Press, 2001), and in such publications as *The New Republic, Barrow Street, Rattapallax, Brilliant Corners,* and *Lit.* A finalist for "Discovery"/ *The Nation Prize*, she is founder and director of the Writers' Night Series for Sarah Lawrence College and a Speaker on Shakespeare for the New York Council for the Humanities. WNET, Public Television, has recently made her a consultant.

David Wojahn's first collection, *Icehouse Lights*, was chosen by Richard Hugo as winner of the Yale Series of Younger Poets prize and published in 1982. The collection was also the winner of the Poetry Society of America's William Carlos Williams Book Award. Other collections, *Glassworks* (1987), *Mystery Train* (1990), *Late Empire* (1994), *The Falling Hour* (1997), and *Spirit Cabinet* (2002), were all published by the University of Pittsburgh Press. He is currently professor of English at Virginia Commonwealth University.

Susan Wood is the author of three books, *Bazaar* (Henry Holt, 1980), *Campo Santo*, winner of the Lamont Prize of the Academy of American Poets (Louisiana State University Press, 1991), and *Asunder*, selected for the National Poetry Series (Penguin, 2001). She is Gladys Louise Fox Professor of English at Rice University and also teaches in the Warren Wilson M.F.A. program for writers.

Baron Wormser is the author of six books of poetry, including *When* (Sarabande Books, 1997) and *Subject Matter* (Sarabande Books, 2004) and the coauthor of two books about teaching poetry, including *Teaching the Art of Poetry: The Moves* (Lawrence Erlbaum Associates, 2000). He lives in Hallowell, Maine.

128

Acknowledgments

Atkins, Cynthia: "Birthday Poem," copyright © 2004, is published with the permission of the author.

Barks, Coleman: "Bill Matthews Coming Along," copyright © 1999, was first published in *Figdust* 1 (1999) and later included in *The Best American Poetry*, 1999, edited by Robert Bly (Scribners, 1999) and is reprinted with the permission of the author.

Baumel, Judith: "Notes for the Elegy," copyright © 2004, is published with the permission of the author.

Beaumont, Jeanne Marie: "After," copyright © 1999, first appeared in *The Gettysburg Review* 12, no. 3 (Autumn 1999) and later in her book *Curious Conduct* (Rochester, N. Y.: BOA, 2004) and is reprinted with the permission of BOA Editions.

Bell, Marvin: "Bill Matthews," copyright © 2004, is published with the permission of the author.

Braggs, Earl S.: "Remembering Bill Matthews," copyright © 2003, appeared in *Crossing Tecumseh Street* (Tallahassee, Fla.: Anhinga Press, 2003) and is reprinted with the permission of Anhinga Press and the author.

Brown, Andrea Carter: "Blues, for Bill," copyright © 2002, was first published in *Ploughshares*, 87, no. 28/1 (Spring 2002) and is reprinted with the permission of the author.

Brown, Harriet: "Unfair," copyright © 2004, is published with the permission of the author.

Burr, Robert: "No Profit," copyright © 2004, is published with the permission of the author.

Cox, Mark: "Pissing Off Robert Frost's Porch" first appeared in *Solo* 5 (2002) and later in *Natural Causes*, copyright © 2004 (University of Pittsburgh Press, 2004) and is reprinted with the permission of University of Pittsburgh Press and the author.

Cramer, Stephen: "Before You," copyright © 2004, is published with the permission of the author.

Feinstein, Sascha: "Matthews in Smoke," copyright © 2004, is published with the permission of the author.

Fischer, Allen C.: "Inspiration," copyright © 2004, first appeared in *The Distillery* (January 2004) and is reprinted with the permission of the author.

Fried, Debra: "Untitled: For Bill Matthews," copyright © 2004, is published with the permission of the author.

Index of Poets and Titles